SOCIAL STUDIES FAIR PROJECTS AND RESEARCH ACTIVITIES

A Comprehensive Guide for Students and Teachers

by Leland Graham
& Isabelle McCoy

Incentive Publications, Inc.
Nashville, Tennessee

Acknowledgements

The authors would like to gratefully acknowledge the assistance and suggestions of the following educators: Deborah Hadaway, Jonathan McCoy, Beverly Moody, Dan Payne and DeKalb County School System, Decatur, GA.

Illustrated by Gayle Harvey
Cover by Marta Drayton
Edited by Jennifer J. Streams

ISBN 0-86530-484-X

2   3   4   5   6   7   8   9   10   08   07   06   05

PRINTED IN THE UNITED STATES OF AMERICA
www.incentivepublications.com

Table of Contents

INTRODUCTION

The majority of *Social Studies Fair Projects and Research Activities* is organized to provide ideas for students and teachers who are looking for social studies fair project ideas. These social studies projects and research activities, which normally take three to eight weeks to complete, are a great way to provide students with some of their most valuable learning experiences based on history, geography, political science, economics, anthropology, and sociology topics.

Some of the featured activities, such as note taking, making an outline, and creating a bibliography, have been designed so that they can be used as individual or group activities; however, other activities involve individual participation. Carefully read the instructions before beginning each chapter.

Since research is an integral part of the social studies project, students will be carefully guided through a step-by-step process on developing the thesis, introductory paragraph, body, and conclusion of their research paper. Included in this book are examples of research papers for teachers to use as guides for students.

A backboard section, also included in this book, is especially important for the actual social studies fair. Even though a student's knowledge and understanding in writing the research paper may be excellent, if the backboard materials are not properly displayed, the project will not receive the proper recognition. To further assist students, the authors have included examples of various types of lettering, design elements, and sample backboard sketches.

The Appendix contains a collection of forms: tips for parents, sample letters to parents and students, a research proposal sheet, a suggested project rubric, judges' score sheets, social studies resources, and a reproducible certificate. Finally, we have included some reproducible title cards which can be printed on card-stock for use on the backboard.

Chapter One

SOCIAL STUDIES DISCIPLINES

Social Studies Disciplines

When beginning work on a Social Studies project, it is important to focus on the various social studies disciplines. On the following pages, there are descriptions of each discipline. Following each discipline are pictures, charts, graphs, maps, or headlines representing a particular discipline that might inspire a topic choice. Chapter Twelve has backboard project examples for each discipline.

History

History, which includes all that has happened to humanity, can be limited to the history of a country; or it can be limited to a group of people, an institution, or a community. History is important to people of different regions and communities, nations, and the world. Because history normally includes analysis and explanation of the events, it is more than a systematic record of events of the past. Topics from the history discipline can often be tied to issues of struggle. Therefore, history is the record of changes in civilizations. When researching history, ask yourself questions such as: "What Were the Effects of the Attack on Pearl Harbor?"
"What Were the Effects of Apartheid in South Africa?"
"The Nile River: Why is it Considered a Cradle of Civilization?"

Geography

The word *geography* is derived from the Greek word *geographia*, which means "a description of the earth." Thus, geography is the study of the earth's surface, humanity's utilization of raw materials and resources, and human behavior as it is influenced by location and other geographic factors. Geography is the study of the relationship between the physical environment and human activity. A geographer describes the earth's surface, the changes that occur in it, the knowledge of its various parts, and the theories of its formation and change. Geographers focus on five fundamental geographic themes: Location, Place, Human-Environmental Interactions, Movement, and Regions.

Social Studies Fair Projects and Research Activities

Political Science

Political science is defined as "the study of politics, government, policy, and the relationship of authority and power." In the different regions of the world, people have found different ways to rule and govern themselves. In the past, governments have developed from the needs of people to organize themselves, defend themselves, or solve an environmental problem. Today, most of the world's governments have a variety of purposes. When researching one of the world's governments, consider these questions: How is the government and its leaders chosen? How is power shared? What are the people's rights? These questions are important because many countries choose to answer them in different ways.

Goldwater   Johnson   Humphrey   Nixon
1964   1968

The Election of 1964

Candidate	Popular Vote	Electoral Vote
Johnson (Democratic)	43,129,566 (61.3%)	486 (90%)
Goldwater (Republican)	27,178,188 (38.6%)	52 (10%)
Others	101,208 (0.1%)	—

The Election of 1968

Candidate	Popular Vote	Electoral Vote
Nixon (Republican)	31,785,480 (43.4%)	301 (55.9%)
Humphrey (Democratic)	31,275,165 (42.7%)	191 (35.5%)
Wallace (American Independent)	9,906,473 (13.5%)	46 (8.6%
Others	218,347 (0.4%)	—

Economics

Economics is concerned mainly with the description, analysis of production, distribution, and consumption of goods and services. The ways in which people use their resources in order to earn a living are known as *economic systems*. People respond to basic economic questions differently; therefore, there are many kinds of economic systems. *Capitalism* is defined as an economic system in which the citizens determine decisions. On the other hand, *communism* is described as an economic system in which goods are owned in common and are available as needed. Who or what determines what people will produce? How do goods get from one place to another? How should goods be shared? Understanding the answers to these questions will naturally help when organizing a social studies project.

Consider one of these fundamental economic concepts for a project: Scarcity; Opportunity Cost and Trade-Offs, Productivity, Economic Systems, Economic Institutions and Incentives, Exchange, Money, and Interdependence.

Economy of the Southern Colonies

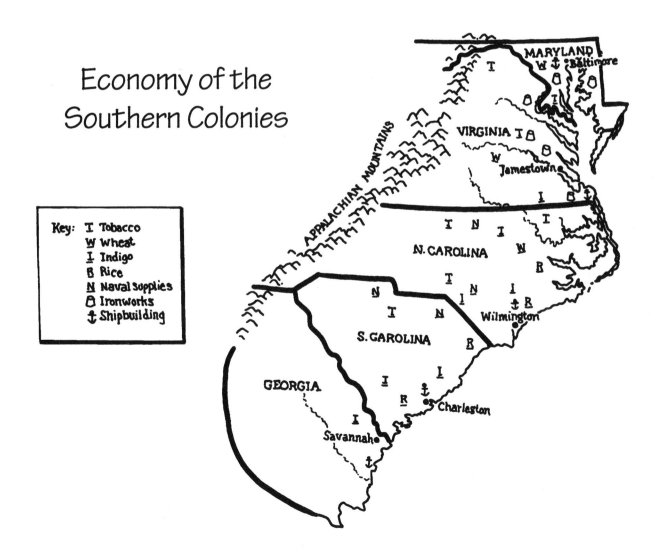

Key:
T Tobacco
W Wheat
I Indigo
B Rice
N Naval Supplies
θ Ironworks
⚓ Shipbuilding

Social Studies Fair Projects and Research Activities

Anthropology

Anthropology is defined as the science of human beings in relation to distribution, origin, classification, and relationships of races. Anthropologists study specific groups of people throughout time and space. The central goal of anthropologists is to explain why groups of people are different from each other. Anthropologists explain why groups have different physical characteristics, speak different languages, use different technologies, and why they think, believe, and act so differently. In writing a research paper for a social studies project, it is important to remember the four main branches of anthropology: *Physical anthropology* is the study of physical characteristics and social behavior of humans past and present. *Archeology* is the study of the material remains of cultures. *Anthropological linguistics* is the study of how groups of people use language. *Cultural anthropology* is the study of different groups' ways of life.

Social Studies Fair Projects and Research Activities

Sociology

Sociology is defined as the science of society, social institutions, and social relationships. To understand a group of people, one needs to know about their ethnic groups, languages, family structure, religions, and customs. An *ethnic group* is defined as a group of people who share a language, history, and/or a place of origin. *Customs* are the practices from the past that people continue to observe. Sociologists study cultures to discover how they vary from place to place. In researching a sociology-centered project, consider how people have changed the land, how they have built cities, and how they use their natural resources.

Sprawl vs. Mother Nature—A Metro-Wide Issue

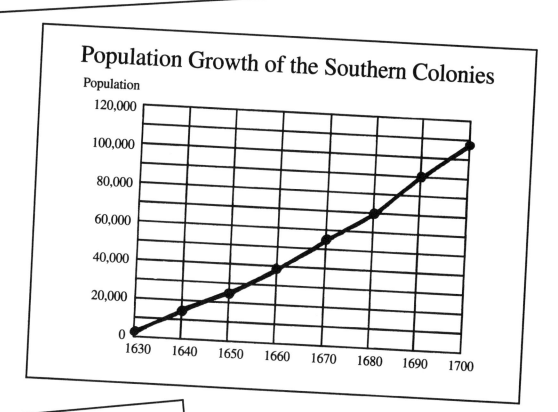

Population Growth of the Southern Colonies

Peace Corps Beefs up its AIDS Work in Africa

Study: Teens Say Guns Easy to Get

Social Studies Fair Projects and Research Activities

Chapter Two

SELECTING A TOPIC

Selecting a Topic

The most important step in writing a research paper is choosing an appropriate topic. In selecting a topic, refer to the six social studies disciplines. Use the guidelines below in choosing a topic.

1. Avoid topics that are limited.

    EXAMPLE: What states were involved in the U.S. Civil War?

    A student cannot write a report on a topic that can be explained in a few words or a sentence.

    BETTER TOPIC: How did the natural resources of states involved in the Civil War affect the outcome of the war?

2. Avoid topics that are too broad.

    EXAMPLE: What happened in the Twentieth Century?

    Topics which are too broad make it impossible to find all the information that is needed to cover the topic adequately.

    BETTER TOPIC: What were the causes of the Great Depression?

3. Some topics have no available information.

    EXAMPLE: Why are some people prejudiced?

    We do not know why some people are prejudiced.

    BETTER TOPIC: Why do employees still experience prejudice in the workplace?

4. Avoid topics which are confusing because we cannot tell what information is requested.

    EXAMPLE: What do people in Korea like?

    We know that the people in Korea may differ in their likes and dislikes.

    BETTER TOPIC: What are the favorite sports of the Korean people?

5. Avoid topics on which people throughout the world cannot agree.

    EXAMPLE: What is the most powerful country in the world?

    Your topic should be supported with facts.

    BETTER TOPIC: Why is the U.S. considered the strongest economic power in the world?

Social Studies Fair Projects and Research Activities

Name _____

Finding a Good Topic to Research

   Teachers sometimes assign topics for students to research in the library. At other times, students can choose topics on their own. If a teacher asks students to choose a topic, students will need to know how to avoid choosing the wrong one. There are at least five kinds of poor topic choices. The following difficulties should be considered before students look for information in the library:

1. **Some topics are too small.**
   Example: *What do you know about your ancestors?*
   A student cannot write a research paper on a topic that can be explained in one or two sentences.

2. **Some topics are too big.**
   Example: *What are the different holidays?*
   Topics which are too big make it impossible for us to find all the information that is necessary to cover the topic adequately.

3. **Some topics simply have no information available.**
   Example: *Why did Christopher Columbus quarrel with his shipmates?*
   We do not know why people behave in a certain manner.

4. **Some topics are confusing because we cannot tell exactly what information is requested.**
   Example: *What do teenagers like?*
   We know that teenagers have different likes and dislikes.

5. **Some topics concern questions in which people throughout the world cannot agree.**
   Example: *What was the world's best invention?*
   People have different opinions, and therefore, cannot agree.

Can you now recall the five problems listed above without looking? List them below.

1. _____

2. _____

3. _____

4. _____

5. _____

Recognizing Poor Topics

The topics below are poor choices for a social studies research paper because of the previously discussed reasons. On the line beneath each topic, write the reason or reasons why it should not be chosen.

1. What country has the most beautiful scenery in the world?

   _____

2. How have people built their cities since early times?

   _____

3. What would be the best way to improve things?

   _____

4. What kind of government does Russia have?

   _____

5. When did Pizarro make his first trip to Latin America?

   _____

6. Why did Alexander the Great like horses?

   _____

7. What kinds of weapons have been used by people since early times?

   _____

8. How tall is the Statue of Liberty?

   _____

Social Studies Fair Projects and Research Activities

Choosing a Topic
(To the Teacher)

Objectives:

1. The students will select a topic and write an appropriate question for their social studies project.

2. The students will conduct a social studies search to determine the availability of materials.

Procedures:

1. In class, have a brainstorming session to list topics of current interest.

   a. Eliminate irrelevant social studies topics.

   b. Eliminate topics that are too broad or too limited.

   c. Eliminate topics that are not original.

   d. Rewrite topics as necessary.

2. Have students continue brainstorming at home in order to select a topic of interest to them.

3. Have students complete Section I of the Proposal Sheet (Appendix page 96).

4. Have students go to the library and search for information to answer the proposed question. Have students list the available sources on the back of the proposal sheet. Do not forget to suggest the Reader's Guide, periodicals, almanacs, government publications, encyclopedias, letters, biographical dictionaries, atlases, and books on the subject. List ideas for conducting surveys, interviews, and observations. Decide on other appropriate social studies methods for gathering information such as visiting areas of significance, taking photos, or writing letters.

5. Have students complete Section II of the Proposal Sheet (see page 96).

6. After approval, have students complete Section III of the Proposal Sheet (see page 96) to outline strategies for answering the questions.

7. Ask students to have a parent or guardian sign the proposal sheet.

Evaluation:

The students will successfully write a research question and an outline of strategies that meets the teacher's approval.

Chapter Three

EXAMPLES
OF
SOCIAL STUDIES
TOPICS

Examples of Social Studies Topics

The following are suggested topics for the social studies fair. Students may select from this list, or they may want to create their own topic.

History

How Much Do You Know About Your School's History?
Our Flag: How Did it Evolve?
What Effect Does a Father Have on the Making of a World Leader?
Why are a Log Cabin and a Farm House Historically Important?
U.S. Involvement in Vietnam: Was it Worth it?
Where are the Historical Markers in Our County?
The Telephone: How has it Changed?
How Much Do you Know About the History of Our City?
How Did Lincoln Get From the Log Cabin to the White House?
What Were the Effects of the Attack on Pearl Harbor?
U.S. Concentration Camps: How Can We Correct this Wrong?
What Was the Puritan Family Lifestyle Like in Colonial America?
The Nile River: Why is it Considered a Cradle of Civilization?
What Were the Effects of Apartheid in South Africa?
What are our National Symbols and Where Did They Originate?

Geography

What Effect Does Acid Rain Have on Our Community?
How is the _____ River Useful to the Metropolitan Area?
How Has Map Making Progressed Through the Centuries?
Why is the Okefenokee Swamp Known as the Land of the Trembling Earth?
How do People Live in the Desert?
Petroleum: How was it Formed and Where is it Found?
Does Cutting Down the Amazon Rainforest Affect Us?
Acid Rain: Is My Country in Danger?
How Does Photography Help in Making Maps?
Can We Save the Ozone Layer From Destruction?
How Useful is the Panama Canal?
Why Should We Protect Our Environment?
How Do These Famous Canals Compare: Panama, Suez, and Erie?

Political Science

The Death Penalty: Should We Abolish It?
How Does our State Government Work?
How Does a Bill Become a Law?
Who Will Be our Next President?
What is the Salt II Treaty?
Should Women Be Drafted?
Voter Apathy: How Does it Affect Election Results?
Should the Driving Age Be 18?
Should Television Cameras Be Allowed in Court?
Have Seat Belt Laws Made a Difference?
The Lottery: Is it Political?
Justice For All? Legal Rights in Our State
What Effect Do Illegal Aliens Have on our Country?
What is an Electoral College and How Does it Work?
What are Some Reasons Why People Don't Vote?
What are Some of the Famous Court Cases and Trials in our State?

Economics

What Are We Going to do When the Gas Runs Out?

State Taxes: Who Shall Pay?

Where Is Your Dollar Going?

What are Penny Stocks?

Shoplifting: Is it Really Worth It?

What are the Causes of Inflation?

How Does Unemployment Affect our Community?

Is Welfare Really Fair in our State?

How has Television Advertising Affected our Lives?

Computer Crime: Is it a Growing Game?

How Does Advertising Affect the Spending Habits of (insert grade) Students at our School?

Are America's Elderly Facing Cost Catastrophe?

Should the Federal Government Deregulate American Business?

Should You do Comparison Shopping at Local Stores?

How Have Computers Changed the Workplace?

How do the Stock Market Crashes of 1929 and 1987 Compare?

Anthropology

What Can Hieroglyphics Tell us About Ancient Egypt?

Prehistoric Life: What Was it Like?

How Did Early Man Live?

Cherokees: What Was Their Lifestyle in the 1800s?

What is the Importance of a Trilobite?

Why Were Ancient Inca Cities Abandoned and Forgotten?

What Role Do Clothing and Physical Attractiveness Play in the Forming of a First Impression?

Did Humankind Originate in Africa?

Who Were the Earliest Citizens of our State?

Creek Indians: What Were Their Customs in the 1700s?

What Was the Lifestyle of the Cliff Dwellers of Mesa Verde?

What Were the Archeological Discoveries at Mission Santa Catalina?

What Will the Mapping of Human Genome Tell Us?

Sociology

The Right To Die: Whose Choice?

How Does Divorce Affect Children?

Is Subliminal Advertising Out to Get You?

I Am Hungry: Where Can I Go to Get Help?

How Safe are Our Vegetables? Meats? Fruits? (Choose One)

Capital Punishment: Is it the Answer?

What are Some Causes of Teenage Suicide?

What Can Be Done About Teenage Pregnancies?

Do Superstitions Influence Behavior?

How Can Types of Music Affect Students' Attitudes and Behavior?

Does Violence on Television Cause Aggressive Behavior in Teens?

Child Abuse: What are the Results?

How Are the Blind Educated?

Prisons: How Have They Changed?

Can Hispanics, or Asians, or Africans, or Europeans (choose one) Adapt to the American Lifestyle?

What are (your school) Students' Favorite Games? TV Shows?

FM Radio: Who Listens? Do You?

Social Studies Fair Projects and Research Activities

Chapter Four

SUGGESTED DEADLINES

Suggested Deadlines

(To the Teacher)

The following suggested due dates may be useful in planning for a successful social studies project.

DUE DATES   **STEPS IN COMPLETING A PROJECT**

Week 1 .... **APPROVED TOPIC AND TITLE**
The title should be in the form of a question.

Week 2 .... **STATEMENT OF PURPOSE**
The purpose states the reason why the topic was selected and what the student plans to prove or explain.

Week 3 .... **OUTLINE OF THE RESEARCH PAPER**
The outline should give both student and teacher a guide as to how the student wishes to present the material.

Week 4 .... **NOTE CARDS**
The note cards should contain one main idea on each card.

Week 5 .... **ROUGH DRAFT**
A parent or guardian should proofread a rough draft before the student submits it to the teacher.

Week 6 .... **ROUGH DRAFT RETURNED**
Students should use the teacher's comments to correct any mistakes.

Week 7 .... **CONCLUSION AND BIBLIOGRAPHY**
The conclusion should restate the purpose, include the findings of the research, and draw conclusions based on the study. The bibliography should include at least four sources.

Week 8 .... **FINAL DRAFT**
The final draft should be typed, not longer than six hundred (600) words, and completely free of errors.

Week 9 .... **BACKBOARD**
The backboard should be neat, colorful, and include the title strips.

Week 10 .... **LOCAL SCHOOL'S SOCIAL STUDIES FAIR**
The fair is held in the gym or media center and is open to all who wish to participate.

23

Chapter Five

FORMAT AND STEPS FOR THE RESEARCH PAPER

Format for the Research Paper

I. Title page

    A. Name of the project

    B. Student's name

    C. Grade level

    D. Discipline

    E. School name

    F. Teacher's name

    G. Date

II. Verification page (Required if student did not type his own paper)

III. Purpose page

    A. Clearly state why the research topic was chosen

    B. Present an overview of the content that will be covered

IV. Methodology page

    A. Outline the steps followed to complete the social studies project

    B. Students may choose to illustrate the process in the form of a timeline

V. Research

    A. Introductory paragraph

        1. Clearly state the general theme

        2. Include basic ideas that will be developed

    B. Research findings

        1. Present information in an orderly, sequential, and convincing manner

        2. Include adequate and properly balanced information

VI. Conclusion page

    A. Argument summary

    B. Key ideas

VII. Credit page (optional)

VIII. Bibliography

Social Studies Fair Projects and Research Activities

Steps for Writing the Research Paper

Prewriting

Think about the project's purpose and audience. Consider these questions: What do I want my reader(s) to learn? How much detail should I include? Who will my reader(s) be? What facts need explanation?

Writing a First Draft

Write: Write the first draft. Remember to follow the outline closely. Write on every other line to leave room for any changes. Write down all the facts without stopping to correct spelling and grammar. Save those changes for later.

Revising

Revising Checklist. Ask the following questions:

• Will the opening make my reader(s) want to know more?

• Does each paragraph begin with a topic sentence?

• Have I included details that support my main ideas?

• Have I explained each fact clearly?

• Does my closing sum up the report?

Revise: Make changes in the first draft. Make the sentences interesting to the readers. A thesaurus can be helpful in finding appropriate words. Have someone else read the report. Ask for their suggestions.

Revise: Can any of the suggestions made by the person who read the paper be used? Do you have any other ideas? Make those changes on the paper.

Proofreading

When proofreading, read the report carefully to check for any mistakes.

Be sure to:

• Use capital letters and punctuation marks.

• Correct any run-on sentences or sentence fragments.

• Use the correct form of every verb.

• Use the correct form of every pronoun.

• Spell all words correctly.

Publishing

- Copy: Write or type the report as neatly as possible.

- Make the cover attractive so that it will coordinate with the entire project.

- Create a bibliography.

- Check: Reread the report to make sure no important information has been left out and no mistakes were made in copying.*

*Adapted from the DeKalb County School System's *Social Studies Fair Handbook*, Decatur, GA.

Proofreading Activity

While writing a research paper, it always helps to proofread, or "proof" what has been written. When proofreading, make sure the punctuation, capitalization, and spelling are correct.

Read the paragraph below. The paragraph has mistakes in punctuation, capitalization, and spelling. First, draw a circle around each mistake. Then, in the space provided, rewrite the paragraph correcting all mistakes. THERE ARE 10 MISTAKES. Can you find all of them?

the origin of furniture as we know it goes back to ancient Egypt. The Egyptians had stools chairs chests tables, and beds; examples of which can be seen in musuems today. They put such everyday objects in the Tombs. They also painted scenes of every day life on the walls of the tombs. Some of these were indoor scenes that showed an abundance of furniture. Many century later, when the sealed tombs were opened examples of both the real furniture and the furniture painted on the walls were found.**

_____

_____

_____

_____

_____

_____

_____

_____

**Adapted from *Building Proofreading Skills*, Incentive Publications, Nashville, TN.

Chapter Six

BIBLIOGRAPHY CARDS AND NOTE TAKING

Bibliography Cards

If a student plans to use information from a particular source (book, encyclopedia, magazine, Internet, interview, surveys, or pamphlets), she must record and keep certain information for the bibliography. The information can be recorded on 3" x 5" index cards, which will make it easier to create a bibliography.

When writing bibliography cards, write a number in the upper right-hand corner of the note card so that you can easily organize and refer to them. Depending on the type of resource used, different information will need to be recorded on the bibliography card.

Record the following information for a book:

1. Name of the author (last name first)

2. Title of the book (underlined)

3. Place of publication (city)

4. Name of the publisher

5. Year of publication (most recent year)

Kusche, Lawrence David. *The Bermuda Triangle Mystery — Solved.* New York: Harper and Row, 1975.

Note: *A comma is placed between the author's last and first names. A period is placed after the author's name and book title. A colon is placed after the city, and a comma is inserted between the publisher and the year. A period is placed after the year.*

Social Studies Fair Projects and Research Activities

Record the following information for an encyclopedia:

1. Name of the author of the article (if there is an author)
2. Title of the article (in quotation marks)
3. Title of the encyclopedia (underlined)
4. Year of publication (edition)

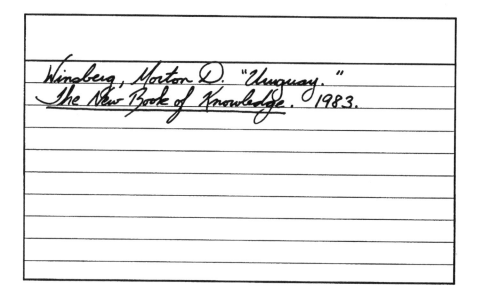

Wingberg, Morton D. "Uruguay."
The New Book of Knowledge. 1983.

Note: If the article has an author, a comma is placed between the author's last and first names. A period is placed after the entire name. A period is placed at the end of article title and before the closing quotation marks. A period is also placed after the name of the encyclopedia.

"United Nations." World Book Encyclopedia.
2000.

Record the following information for a magazine or newspaper:
1. Name of the author (if one is given)
2. Title of the article (in quotation marks)
3. Name of the magazine or newspaper (underlined)
4. Date of the magazine or newspaper
5. Page number(s) of the article

Gordon, James S. "What's the Truth About the Bermuda Triangle?" Reader's Digest. July 1, 1995: 75-79.

Note: *A comma is placed between the author's last and first names. A period is placed after the entire name. A comma is placed between the month and year. The date is followed by a colon. A period is placed after the page number(s). If the article begins on one page but is continued on a non-consecutive page, a comma is inserted between the page numbers (e.g., 83, 86, 94). If the article appears on consecutive pages, a hyphen is inserted between the page numbers (e.g., 83–86).*

"Amazing Amazon Region." New York Times. Jan. 12, 1981: Sec. B, p. 11.

Note: *The above example illustrates an unsigned newspaper article. The punctuation remains the same.*

Social Studies Fair Projects and Research Activities

Record the following information for a computer reference:

If referencing a magazine article from the computer, follow the format for writing a bibliography card for a magazine article. If referencing an encyclopedia from the computer, follow the format for writing an encyclopedia bibliography card.

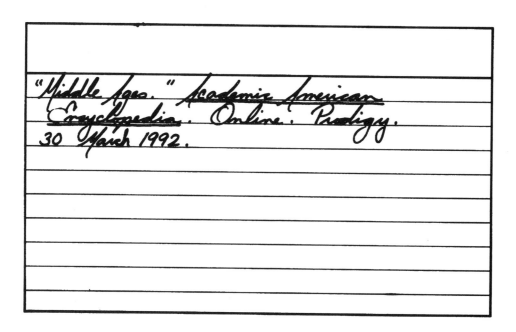

Note: Bibliography cards need to be made if dictionaries, atlases, almanacs, audio tapes, videotapes, television programs, movies, interviews, letters, surveys, or the Internet are used. Ask a teacher for assistance.

Note Taking

Note taking is a shortcut for writing down information that has been read and needs to be remembered. Taking notes is a very important process when writing a research paper. One cannot expect to remember all that is read. Some writers choose to take notes on note sheets such as the sample note sheet on page 34. Many writers decide to take notes on index cards or slips of paper, using a different card for each main idea. Here are some helpful hints for preparing note cards:

1. Write a word or phrase that summarizes the information on the top left-hand corner of the note card.

2. Write the number from the bibliography card that lists the source of the information used on the top right-hand corner of the note card.

3. Write the information on the note cards in your own words (paraphrase). Write only one idea per note card. Do not write notes from two sources on the same card.

4. If using quoted material, write the material enclosed in quotation marks. Limit the use of direct quotes when taking notes.

5. At the bottom of every note card, write the page number from the source in which the information was found.*

```
Contributions to our country                    6
_____

_____

Ben Franklin was assistant to the
Postmaster General. He organized
the first postal delivery system.
_____

_____

_____

                                         p. 36
```

*Adapted from *How To Write A Great Research Paper*, Incentive Publications, Nashville, TN.

Social Studies Fair Projects and Research Activities

Sample Note Sheet

Name _____   Date _____

Source _____

Title of Source: _____

Author's Name: _____

Publisher: _____

Copyright Year: _____

Place of Publication: _____

Page Numbers: _____

Title of Research: _____

Write your notes IN YOUR OWN WORDS:

_____

_____

_____

_____

_____

_____

_____

_____

_____

_____

_____

_____

_____

_____

_____

If needed, continue your notes on another sheet of paper.

Name _____

Practice Note Taking

Use your judgment in choosing the most important and least important statements.
Read the article carefully and then answer the questions that follow.

Benjamin Franklin, An Extraordinary Man

Benjamin Franklin, one of the most extraordinary men in American history, was the fifteenth child in a family of seventeen children. Because Benjamin's father was a candle maker, Benjamin had to drop out of school very early to help his father in his work; however, this did not keep him from stretching his mind in many directions.

Benjamin did so many interesting things that it is difficult to list them all. After studying electricity, he invented the lightning rod. He also invented bifocal glasses that allowed people to see both near and far. The Franklin stove, another of his inventions, made the heating of homes much more efficient and economical. In addition to showing farmers how to improve acidic soil by using lime, he also taught sailors how to calm stormy seas by pouring oil on the surface of the water.

Franklin served his country in many ways. As assistant to the Postmaster General of the Colonies, he organized the first postal delivery system. As Minister to France, he helped greatly in winning the Revolutionary War. He also did much to assure the success of the Constitutional Convention by offering the compromise amendment which prevented the break-up of the new governing body.

As a writer and educator, Franklin developed and published the *Pennsylvania Gazette* which carried the first cartoons and maps ever printed in newspapers. His interest in education led him to start an academy which offered high school studies. This school later developed into the University of Pennsylvania.

Which two contributions were the two most important to the establishment of our country?

1. _____

2. _____

Which two accomplishments were the least important to the establishment of our country?

1. _____

2. _____

Which contribution by Franklin was the most important to people's health?

_____

Social Studies Fair Projects and Research Activities

Name _____

Practice Note Taking

When taking notes, begin by skimming the material in order to get a general idea of the content. When reading the material for the second time, read more carefully in order to find the main points and details. Instead of writing complete sentences, make brief notes.

On the right side of this page, take notes on the article below. Remember to use brief notes instead of complete sentences. Check the article for main ideas, cue words, and punctuation. Remember to use quotation marks for direct quotes.

Uruguay	Your Notes
Uruguay, one of the smallest of the South American republics, is located on the east coast of the continent between Brazil and Argentina. A land of gently rolling hills and temperate climate, it is the only South American country with no large uninhabited areas.	
At first, most of Uruguay's settlers came from Spain. People later arrived from many other countries. In the mid 1800's, there was an influx of British settlers. Blacks immigrated to Uruguay from Brazil soon after Brazil abolished slavery. Other Europeans have also settled in Uruguay.	
Uruguay is one of the smallest and most unified countries in South America, but its people follow two distinct ways of life: rural and urban. The rural life is typified by the gauchos— the colorful cattle or sheep herders of the region. Urban life in Uruguay is similar to that found in Europe. Careful appearance and behavior, good manners, and a love of culture are important to their way of life.	

Chapter Seven

MAKING AN OUTLINE

Making an Outline

Making an outline will make writing a research paper easier. Think of the outline as the writing plan. An outline helps the writer sort out the main ideas and the supporting facts. The ideas and supporting facts were recorded on the note cards during the research phase of the project. The outline will help plan the best order for those ideas.

1. Write the title of the paper across the top of the page.

2. Place a Roman numeral and a period before each main topic.

3. When dividing the main topic into subtopics, be sure to place the A directly underneath the first letter of the first word of the main topic.

4. If a main topic is divided, it must have at least two subtopics.

5. If using words or phrases instead of complete sentences in the outline, do not place a period after a main topic or subtopic.

6. Always begin the main topic and subtopic with a capital letter and capitalize any proper nouns.

7. An outline should use parallel structure. In other words, the same kind of word or phrase should be used.

    Incorrect use: I. Early Childhood of Ben Franklin

    A. Education

    B. He helped his father with candle making.

The example is incorrect because it does not use parallel structure. The topic is a phrase, the first subtopic is a word, and the second subtopic is a sentence. The following example shows an outline written in words.

The Life and Times of John Quincy Adams

I. Early Life
    A. Childhood
    B. Education
    C. Lawyer and Writer
II. Political and Public Career
    A. Diplomat
    B. U.S. Senator
    C. Secretary of State
III. Adams' Administration (1825-1829)
    A. Democratic-Republican Party Split
    B. Congress Rebuff
    C. White House Life

Social Studies Fair Projects and Research Activities

Practice Outlining

Read the story below and then fill in the outline under the major headings.

The Growth of the Roman Empire

Nearly 3,000 years ago, ancient people were tending their simple farms in a region of Italy that later became a part of Rome. Rome, in turn, became the center of the Roman Empire. These early people began trading in one of the valleys between the seven hills where the city of Rome gradually developed. This valley between the hills became known as the market place, or forum.

As Rome grew, the Romans took over more land. They conquered tribes nearby and then built walls to protect the lands they had conquered. One of the early kings, Servius, built a wall entirely around the city to keep enemies out. The Romans were able to conquer many different tribes of people because they were able to work together very well. They were proud of their accomplishments.

The Romans sent armies south to conquer the southern part of Italy. Gradually these same armies made their way across the Mediterranean Sea to Africa where they conquered the great city of Carthage. The land in Africa was ideal for growing wheat. It was not long before Roman ships were sailing back and forth across the Mediterranean Sea, carrying wheat from North Africa to feed the people of Rome. The Romans conquered lands at the eastern and western ends of the Mediterranean Sea as well.

The Romans were great builders. They constructed pipelines known as aqueducts to carry fresh water into their cities, and they built stone roads and bridges to help in the movement of goods and armies from one part of the empire to another. The Romans also constructed huge walls to protect their boundaries. Many of these aqueducts, roads, bridges, and walls can be seen today. In Rome itself, the Romans built beautiful temples, stadiums, and other public buildings. Thousands of people go to Rome each year to see the remains of these great buildings.*

I. The Founding of Rome

   A. _____

   B. _____

II. Changes That Took Place as Rome Grew

   A. _____

   B. _____

III. Roman Accomplishments in Building

   A. _____

   B. _____

   C. _____

*Adapted from DeKalb County School System's *Social Studies Fair Handbook*, Decatur, GA.

Social Studies Fair Projects and Research Activities

Name _____

Further Outline Practice

To further test your knowledge of outlines, parts of two outlines are given below. The outlines are in scrambled order. For the first outline, the form is supplied for you. For the second outline, you are on your own.

Government
English
Homes
Language
Episcopalian
Manufacturing
People
Baptist
Economy
Gaelic
Natural Resources
Church of Scotland
Lifestyles
Agriculture
Recreation
Religion

Scotland

I.
II. People
  A.
    1.
    2.
  B.
    1.
    2.
  C.
    1.
    2.
    3.
III. Economy
  A. Natural Resources
  B.
  C.

Suggestion: It might be wise to put in the Roman numerals first for each of the two main topics and leave space for the subtopics under each main topic.

Chester A. Arthur

Boyhood
Political Growth
Early Life
Election
Legal Career
Family
Opposition
Political and Public Career

Chapter Eight

WRITING THE RESEARCH PAPER

Writing the Research Paper

Now that the note cards and preliminary outline are completed, it is time to write the first draft of your research paper. When beginning to write the first draft, concentrate only on putting the main ideas on paper. Do not be concerned about spelling, grammar, and punctuation. The following evaluation guidelines will help as the first draft is being written.

Objective: Write the thesis statement, stating the purpose for this research study. (Please understand that it is a broad answer to questions posed in the paper.)

Introduction: The introduction may be one or two paragraphs. The purpose of the introduction is to grab the reader's attention.

Body: The next step is to separate the note cards according to the main topics and subtopics as shown in the outline. Begin to read the note cards. If it is discovered that there are two or more note cards with similar information, place them together. Next, read the cards for logical order. Turn the note cards over as they are used in the draft. Do not discard any note cards; they may be used later.

Documentation: Be sure the sources are properly documented in the research paper. Unless the teacher requests a different format, use the MLA format for documentation. When using a word-for-word quotation, be sure to enclose it in quotation marks and identify the source.

Conclusion: The conclusion, which signals the end of the paper, may be one or two paragraphs and should restate the thesis. It should include any opinions of the author based on the research and study prescribed in the report. Do not include any new information or documentation.

Here are examples of a good thesis statement, introductory paragraph, and conclusion.

Sample Thesis Statement

The Cape Hatteras Lighthouse should be saved so that future generations can enjoy this historical landmark.

Sample Introductory Paragraph

The Cape Hatteras Lighthouse, the tallest in America, has lighted the dangerous Diamond Shoals off Cape Hatteras, North Carolina, for 116 years. It is now being threatened by the treacherous waves and erosion of the Atlantic Ocean and could be destroyed by a major storm. This report will discuss ways in which the lighthouse can be saved and whether tax dollars should be spent to save it.

Sample Conclusion

Experts still disagree over which is the best alternative to protect the Cape Hatteras Lighthouse, but most agree that erosion will eventually topple the lighthouse unless something is done. The ocean could topple the lighthouse in the next ten to fifteen years. Many people believe that tax dollars should not be spent to save the lighthouse and that private dollars should be raised to pay for the reconstruction. The Save the Cape Hatteras Lighthouse Committee is determined to save the lighthouse and has raised $500,000 of private money for that purpose.

There are alternatives which experts believe could protect the lighthouse from erosion. The cost would be expensive, and no one is sure that any of the alternatives will work. The lighthouse is a popular North Carolina historical landmark. Thousands of people visit the Cape Hatteras National Seashore and the lighthouse every year. Therefore, in my opinion, a special effort should be made to save the lighthouse for future generations.

Social Studies Fair Projects and Research Activities

Practice Rewriting the Introductory Paragraph

While writing the introductory paragraph, please keep in mind that it is important to state the reason(s) for choosing this topic and to explain what will be proven in the research paper.

Directions: Edit the following first draft paragraph. While rewriting the paragraph, feel free to change any of the words, place the sentences in a more logical order, and remove any sentences that do not agree with the main topic. Also, correct any errors in spelling, capitalization, and punctuation.

I also wanted to know if my personlity fits in with my birth order. this topic was chosen because I have always been intersted in Birth order and Personality In this report, I will discuss what many studies prove about birth order and what many Psychologists think about birth order. Does birth order determine personality. Only children are the only children that parents give birth to. I will try to determine how well prevous findings predict ones personality and also try to discover new personality traits that follow the order of one's birth.

_____

_____

_____

_____

_____

_____

_____

_____

_____

_____

_____

Social Studies Fair Projects and Research Activities

Practice Rewriting a Conclusion

Remember that the concluding paragraph(s) should restate the thesis and should include any opinions of the writer based on the research and study described in the report.

Read the following conclusion. Feel free to change any of the words, place the sentences in a more logical order, and remove any sentences that do not agree with the main topic. Also, correct any errors in spelling, capitalization, and punctuation.

It is really more a museum for people to walk through and leave knowing more about the man and our country during the years that he was president. The purpose of a Presidential Library is to give visitors to the librery a better understanding of the particuler president, of the office of the President, and the American political system? each year teachers students and others come from all over the country to use the materials in the library for research purposes. The Presidential Records Act of 1978 made it a requirement for presidents to donate official papers to the government. A presidential library is unlike any other library.

_____

_____

_____

_____

_____

_____

_____

_____

_____

_____

Practice Writing a Thesis Statement

Complete the following by writing a thesis statement for each question.

1. Question: Can we save the ozone layer from destruction?

    Thesis: _____

    _____

2. Question: Should women be drafted in the armed services?

    Thesis: _____

    _____

3. Question: What can be done about teenage pregnancies?

    Thesis: _____

    _____

4. Question: The Nile River: Why is it considered a cradle of civilization?

    Thesis: _____

    _____

5. Question: Shoplifting: Is it really worth it?

    Thesis: _____

    _____

6. Question: Did humankind originate in Africa?

    Thesis: _____

    _____

Name _____

Writing the Thesis Statement and Introductory Paragraph

In the space provided, write a thesis statement and an introductory paragraph. Continue writing the first draft on notebook paper.

_____
Title of Research Paper

Thesis Statement: _____

_____

_____

Introductory Paragraph: _____

_____

_____

_____

_____

_____

_____

_____

_____

_____

_____

_____

_____

_____

Social Studies Fair Projects and Research Activities

Name _____

Writing the Conclusion

In the space provided, write your conclusion. Remember that the conclusion can be one or two paragraphs. It should restate the thesis and include any opinions that support the thesis.

_____

_____

_____

_____

_____

_____

_____

_____

_____

_____

_____

_____

_____

_____

_____

_____

_____

Chapter Nine

PREPARING A FINAL BIBLIOGRAPHY

Preparing a Final Bibliography

In Chapter Six, "Bibliography Cards and Note Taking," you learned how to create bibliography cards for the sources used to write a research paper. Those cards will be helpful when creating a final bibliography list, which is a list of the sources used for the research paper. When making a bibliography list:

1) put the list in alphabetical order according to the author's last name (if the author is not given, alphabetize by the first word in the title),

2) underline the title of books, encyclopedias, newspapers, and magazines, and

3) record the city, publishing company, and date of publication.

The bibliography should be placed on the last page of the research paper. Each final bibliographical entry should resemble the following examples:

Book with a single author:

Burgess, John E. <u>Watching Washington Grow into Manhood</u>.
    New York: Franklin Thomas Publishing, 1948.

Newspaper article–unsigned:

"Cutting Down the Cherry Tree." <u>New York Times</u>. Feb. 10, 1981:
    Sec. C, p. 24.

Magazine with an author listed:

Gordan, Lawrence. "What's the Truth about George Washington?"
    <u>George</u>. July, 1995: 24–29.

Pamphlet:

"Mt. Vernon." <u>Presidents in Review</u>. Washington, D.C.: U.S.
    Government Printing Office, 1960.

Book with more than one author:

Smith, Joseph and Fred Stipple. <u>The Life and Times of George</u>
    <u>Washington</u>. Atlanta: Gerrard Publishing, 2000.

Social Studies Fair Projects and Research Activities   Copyright ©2001 by Incentive Publications, Inc., Nashville, TN.

Encyclopedia article–unsigned:

"Washington, George." <u>World Book Encyclopedia</u>. 1964.

Accessed through a computer service:

"Death Penalty." <u>Academic Encyclopedia</u>. Online. Prodigy, 7 July 1999.

Book with an editor:

Drake, Charlton, ed. <u>The Death Penalty</u>. New York: Charlesbridge
    Publishing, 1970.

Encyclopedia with a signed article:

Edwards, Jonathan. "Death Penalty." <u>Encyclopedia Britannica</u>.
    14th ed. 1985.

A television program:

"Is the Death Penalty Fair?" "48 Hours," ABC, Jane Pauley.
    February 22, 2000.

Periodically published database on CD-Rom:

Johnson, Cynthia. "Understanding the Death Penalty." <u>U.S. News &
    World Report</u>. August 5, 1989: 20–27. CD-Rom. Fall 1989.

Publication on a diskette:

Madison, Martha. "Debate: The Death Penalty." Diskette. Atlanta:
    Graham Publishing, 1999.

Electronic Mail (E-mail):

McNeil, Robert. Mississippi River Research Project Results.
    [Online] Available e-mail: <u>student3@tuckerhigh.edu</u> from
    <u>ert@information.512.ga.us, July 24, 2000</u>.

Subject encyclopedia:

Thomas, Joseph. "Thurgood Marshall: Opinions on the Death
    Penalty." <u>Biographical Dictionary</u>. Ed. Charles Gillispie. Vol. VII.
    New York: McCoy Publishing, 1987. 89–91.

Writing Bibliographical Entries

When writing a research paper, it is necessary to include a bibliography at the end. The bibliography is a list of all the sources used when gathering information for the paper. Bibliographies follow a special format and list important information about the sources. Write bibliographical entries for the sources listed below. Use the example as a guide.

Example: "Presidential Libraries: Where Tourists, Scholars Brush Elbows."
<u>U.S. News & World Report</u>. July 11, 1977, pp. 23–25.

1. A book called The Life and Times of Judge Judy was written by John Law Your and published by Jurisprudence Publishers, New York, in 1999.

   _____

   _____

2. Army Ants was an article written by Clark Roach for the Orkin Encyclopedia, Vol. A, and published in 1998.

   _____

   _____

3. A book called Worms—Love 'Em or Leave 'Em was written by Rigg Lee and published by Pete Moss Publishers, New York, in 1982.

   _____

   _____

4. D. A. D'Longlegs interviewed by A. T. Leggs at 10 A.M. on October 26, 1999 in Marshy Bogg Swamp, Seattle, WA.

   _____

   _____

5. Social Studies Teachers Can Win $5,000 Prize was an article found in the CD News-Bank, <u>The News & Observer</u> on September 27, 1996: B1. It was written by Thomas Jefferson Smith.

_____

_____

6. The book, Living Without Electricity, was written by Steven Scott and Kenneth Pellman in 1990. It was published by Good Books in Pittsburgh.

_____

_____

7. Appearing in Vol. 22 of the Encyclopedia Britannica in the 1963 edition was an article on "Turkey," found on pages 193–205.

_____

_____

8. I received an e-mail through Usenet entitled The Technical German on September 7, 1994. Thomas Michael Shaumann wrote it on August 5, 1994. It was received from Newsgroup comp.educ.languages.natural.

_____

_____

9. Censorship, a book with David L. Bender as the editor, was written in 1985 in St. Paul and published by Greenhaven Press.

_____

_____

Social Studies Fair Projects and Research Activities

Bibliography Practice

Jennifer needs help writing a bibliographic list. She used the sources listed in the paragraph below while writing her research report: *Does Birth Order Determine Personality?*.

    In the book *Family Constellation* written by Walter Toman, Jennifer found information. The book was published in New York by Springer Publishing Company, Inc. in 1976. In *The Birth Order Book* published by Dell Publishing Company, Inc., in New York, she found information on pages 14-152. This book was written by Kevin Leman and published in 1985. Jennifer also read *Sky Magazine* in September 1985 where she found an article on pages 145-148 entitled "Personality by Position." In 1983, Cecile Ernst and Jules Angst wrote the book *Birth Order* which was published by Springer-Verlag in Berlin. Finally, Jennifer found an article in <u>Encyclopedia Americana</u> entitled "Birth Order," which appeared in 1987 in the B Volume on pages 77–79.

Bibliography

_____

_____

_____

_____

_____

_____

_____

_____

_____

_____

_____

_____

Writing the Final Bibliography

It is now your turn to write a bibliography for your paper. Use the space provided below. Remember: When making the bibliography list: 1) put the list in alphabetical order according to the author's last name (if the author is not given, alphabetize by the first word in the title); 2) underline the title of books, encyclopedias, newspapers, and magazines; and 3) record the city, publishing company, and date of publication. Use pp. 50–51 for reference.

Bibliography

_____

_____

_____

_____

_____

_____

_____

_____

_____

_____

_____

_____

_____

_____

Social Studies Fair Projects and Research Activities

Chapter Ten

SAMPLE RESEARCH PAPERS

Sample Research Papers

It is now time to write the final draft of the social studies research paper. Before beginning to write or type the paper, remember that it must be complete and neat. Consider using a computer to write the social studies research paper. The computer saves a great deal of time and allows for saving and retrieving of a document. It also allows writers to edit or make corrections quickly and easily. In this final stage, proofreading is crucial. This is the time to check for spelling, punctuation, capitalization, organization, clarity, word choice, and parallel structure.

When preparing a final draft, consider the following guidelines:

1. If handwriting the paper, use lined paper.

2. Use blue or black if writing the paper by hand.

3. Do not skip lines when writing on lined paper; however, when typing a paper, double-space it.

4. For both typing and handwriting, allow one inch for the top, bottom, left, and right margins.

5. The beginning of each paragraph should *always* be indented.

6. When preparing a title page, remember to include the title of the paper, the discipline, your name, the teacher's name, and the date.

7. Number the pages consecutively in the upper right-hand corner of each page. Do not number the first page.

8. A research paper should be organized as follows: title page, outline, thesis, introduction paragraph(s), body, conclusion, bibliography, and credit page (if applicable).

9. Do not discard any materials (bibliography cards, outline, note cards, or drafts) because you may be asked to submit these items to the teacher.

57

On the following pages, there are samples of the final handwritten paper (with marginal information) of Jonathan McCoy's *The Amish: Who Are They?* and the final typewritten paper (with marginal information) of Jon Michael Nordan's *What Is A Presidential Library?*

Title Page

The title page contains 1) the title of the research paper; 2) the social studies discipline (geography, history, political science, anthropology, sociology, or economics); 3) the writer's name; 4) the teacher's name; and 5) the date.

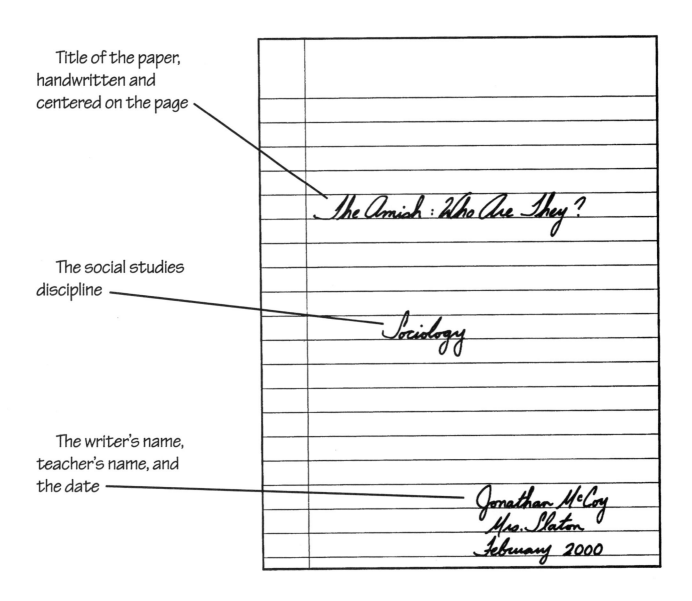

Title of the paper, handwritten and centered on the page

The Amish: Who Are They?

The social studies discipline

Sociology

The writer's name, teacher's name, and the date

Jonathan McCoy
Mrs. Slaton
February 2000

Final Outline

Title of paper →

Thesis statement →

Main topic →

Subtopics →

Details →

Main topic →

Subtopics →

Details →

Note: All main, subtopics, and details have parallel structure.

The Amish: Who Are They?

Thesis: The Amish, a strict religious group, live in much the same way as their seventeenth century ancestors did.

I. Amish History
  A. Switzerland
    1. Joseph Amman
    2. Persecution
  B. United States
    1. William Penn
    2. Freedom
II. Amish Today
  A. Lifestyle
    1. Homes
    2. Conveniences
  B. Religion
  C. Education
    1. Subjects
    2. Teachers
  D. Customs
    1. Clothing
    2. Funerals
  E. Agriculture
    1. Farmhouse
    2. Equipment
    3. Crops

The margins are in keeping with the guidelines.

The thesis is clearly stated.

The paragraphs have been properly indented.

If you drive through Lancaster County, Pennsylvania, you will see horse-drawn buggies sharing the road with modern forms of transportation. This is what I saw on my vacation to Pennsylvania. I learned that the Amish were the people who drove these buggies. The Amish, a strict religious group, live in much the same way as their seventeenth century ancestors did.

The Amish have a different way of life than anyone around them. The Amish have always lived by their religious beliefs and followed the teachings of the Bible. The Amish acquired their name from Joseph Amman. Amman and his followers stressed a simple life and strict church discipline. The Amish believe in kicking out excommunicated members.

The Amish originated in seventeenth century Switzerland. William Penn invited them to

60

Notice the page number is in the upper right-hand corner.

Observe the sentence structure and the organization.

Sentence variety and word choice.

the New World to settle in Pennsylvania. They welcomed the opportunity to escape religious persecution to live in a place of peace. From 1710 to the end of the eighteenth century, the Amish settled along the streams and fertile valleys of southeastern Pennsylvania. Today, the largest population of Amish is in Ohio. Approximately 82,000 Amish live throughout the United States.

Last summer my family and I visited an Amish community in Lancaster County, Pennsylvania. We toured a village where the homes were unlike most Americans' homes. Amish homes do not have radios, television, electricity, or any other modern conveniences. Coal, gas, or oil powered heaters are their only sources of heat. The Amish do have gas-powered refrigerators. Kerosene or naptha burning lamps are their main sources of light. The Amish don't have running water other than a small kitchen water pump. Other water must be pumped from an outdoor pump and then carried into the house.

Meals are prepared and eaten in the

Social Studies Fair Projects and Research Activities

kitchen, the largest and most used room in the house. The kitchen is also used for playing games, reading, sewing, and doing schoolwork. All rooms, especially the kitchen, are kept spotless.

The Amish worship on Sunday. They are a Christian group. Their services are sometimes held in members' homes or in a barn. They begin their services at eight in the morning and finish at noon. Men and women sit on wooden benches on different sides of the room. Their worship services are attended by twenty-five to thirty families. The host family serves lunch to the congregation.

School is held in a one room schoolhouse. Amish children study spelling, English, penmanship, reading, grammar, arithmetic, social studies, and the Bible. Students attend school from kindergarten to eighth grade. The Amish do not see a need for education beyond eighth grade, since they farm for a living. The school teachers are usually young, unmarried Amish women, who have apprenticed in a classroom for two years, but also have only an eighth grade education. Amish children

Observe the correct use of punctuation.

Ideas closely
follow the
outline.

do not attend public school because parents do not want their children influenced by those not of their faith.

One way to identify the Amish is by their dress. Most Amish clothing is homemade by Amish women, who are taught to sew at an early age. The women usually wear long, black, blue, or green dresses with aprons worn over the dresses. If a woman is married, the apron is black, but if she is unmarried, the apron is white. White caps are also worn but jewelry or colorful clothes are not allowed. Men dress in black or dark suits. Suspenders without buttons hold up their pants. Zippers are not allowed. Hook and eye fasteners are used. A black felt hat or straw hat completes their wardrobe. Married men must have beards but not mustaches. Boys and girls dress like their parents.

Amish funerals are rather standard. Both men and women are buried in white. When a person

Social Studies Fair Projects and Research Activities

Note the sentence structure and the organization.

dies the funeral is held three days later, unless that day is a Sunday. The wooden coffin is taken to the cemetery in a horse-drawn hearse. Because no flowers are laid on the grave, the only marker is a tombstone. The Amish believe in life after death. Their afterlife is based on their earthly life.

Ownership of a farm is the primary goal of an Amish family. The Amish work hard on their farms. They take pride in them. Their farms are neat but not very large. Amish farm equipment has steel wheels and is powered by horses, mules, or both. If neighbors need equipment, Amish farmers will lend it to them. The Amish crops usually consist of corn, barley, wheat, and a variety of vegetables. Tobacco is sometimes raised as a cash crop.

Through my research, I have learned that the Amish

Social Studies Fair Projects and Research Activities

Conclusion

Has Jonathan restated his thesis?

Notice how the writer has given his opinion in the conclusion.

are deeply religious; they dress simply; they do not use modern conveniences; and they are dedicated to farming. Although the outside world has changed rapidly, the Amish do not use new technology unless it does not conflict with their basic beliefs. The Amish live in much the same way as their seventeeth century ancestors did. In my opinion, the Amish people live a simple but interesting life.

Social Studies Fair Projects and Research Activities

The word *bibliography* is capitalized and centered on the last page.

The entries are in alphabetical order.

The second and third lines are properly indented.

Bibliography

Amish Country. Gettysburg: IEM, Inc.

Denlinger, A. Martha. Real People.
Scottdale: Herald Press, 1986.

Hostetler, John A. Amish Life.
Scottdale: Herald Press, 1983.

Scott, Stephen and Kenneth Pellman.
Living Without Electricity. Philadelphia:
Good Books, 1990.

Title Page

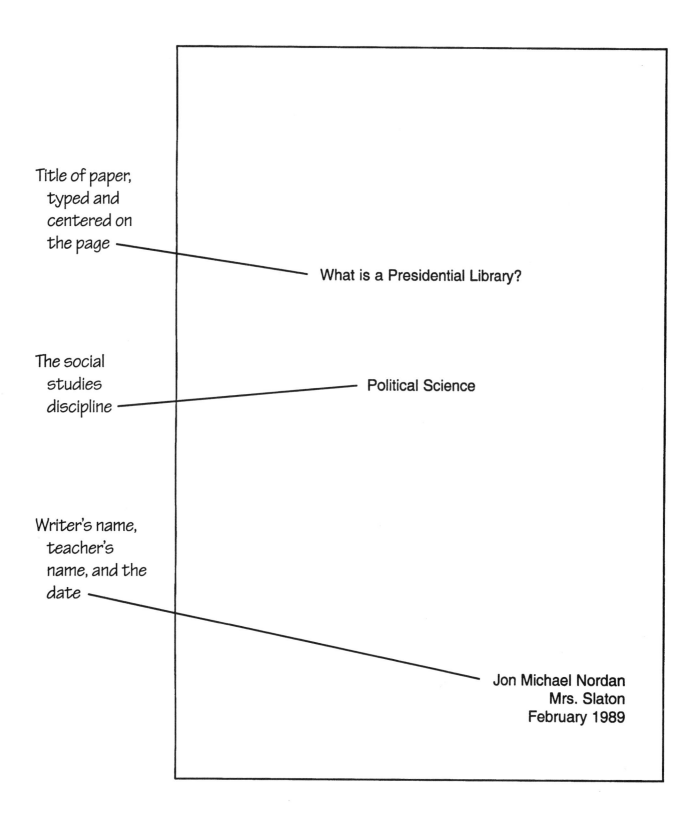

Title of paper, typed and centered on the page ——— What is a Presidential Library?

The social studies discipline ——— Political Science

Writer's name, teacher's name, and the date ———

Jon Michael Nordan
Mrs. Slaton
February 1989

Social Studies Fair Projects and Research Activities

Final Outline

Title of Paper

Thesis Statement

What is a Presidential Library?

Thesis: A presidential library is a time capsule that one can visit and when you leave, you will know more about the man himself and our country during the years that he was president.

Main Topic

I. Purpose

II. History

III. Presidents

Subtopics

    A. Roosevelt

    B. Others

IV. Components

Main Topic

    A. Documents

    B. Donations

    C. Papers

        1. Political

        2. Military

Subtopics

    D. Audio-visuals

    E. Heirlooms

        1. Furniture

        2. Artwork

Details

    G. Gifts

        1. Friends

        2. Foreign Dignitaries

        3. Handicrafts

V. Importance

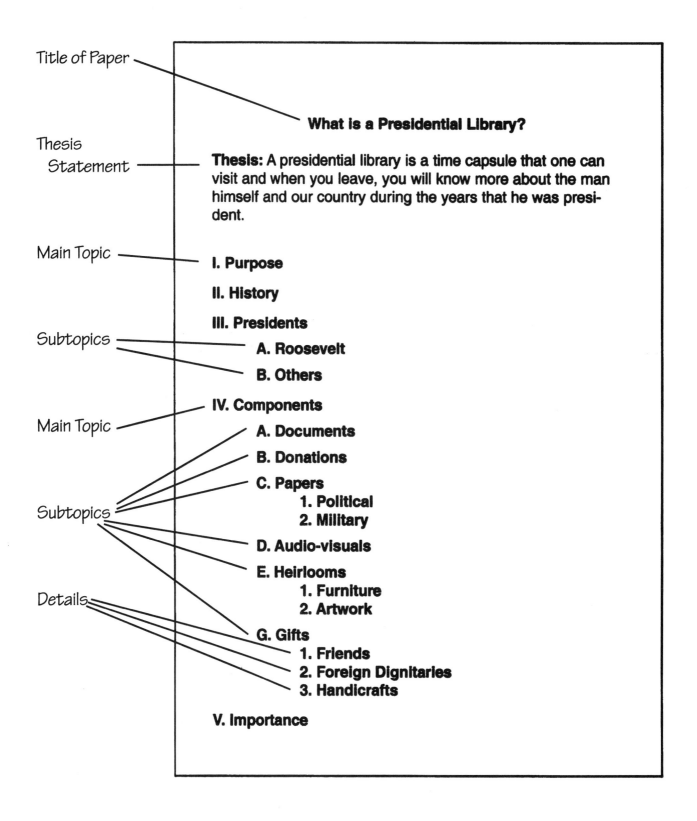

Social Studies Fair Projects and Research Activities

Body

The topic is restated. —

The thesis is clearly stated. —

The paragraphs are properly indented. —

What is a presidential library? A presidential library is like a time capsule you can visit and when you leave, you will know more about the man and our country, during the years that he was president. Inside, you can find important documents records, and letters. These are referred to as the Presidential Papers. You will also find audio-visual materials, campaign memorabilia, and gifts to the first family.

The Presidential Libraries System consists of eight archival and museum complexes. Each one contains the historical materials that document the career of a president, and each is located in an area of the country associated with the president's life. The system exists in order to preserve and make available research materials relating to the modern American Presidency. It functions as a unit of the National Archives and Records Administration (NARA), the agency of the Federal Government that is responsible for maintaining the government's permanently valuable records.

The Presidential Libraries Act of 1955 was passed by Congress to enable Presidents to donate official papers to the

Social Studies Fair Projects and Research Activities

2

government. The Presidential Records Act of 1978 made it a

requirement for Presidents to donate official papers to the gov-

ernment. Many of the collections of presidential papers have

been lost or destroyed. Of the first thirty-five Presidents' papers,

substantial collections exist for only twenty-six. The Presidents

whose papers have been largely dispersed or destroyed are

Monroe, Harrison, Tyler, Taylor, Fillmore, Pierce, Grant, Arthur,

and Harding. Some items from these Presidents are scattered in

various public and private collections. There is no way now of

putting together any record of their activities.

Franklin D. Roosevelt established the first presidential

library in 1939. He thought it was important for a president's

papers and documents to be preserved and made available to

the public. However, he was actually following a practice start-

ed by George Washington and continued by subsequent pres-

idents.

In the late 1930's, Roosevelt proposed and Congress

approved a plan for a joint private and public effort to

establish the Franklin D. Roosevelt Library. Friends of the President formed a non-profit corporation that raised enough funds from the 28,00 contributors to construct a library in Hyde Park, New York. The Roosevelt Library proved so satisfactory as an instrument for preserving presidential materials that Congress passed the Presidential Libraries Act.

Eight presidential libraries are already in existence and two others have been started. Richard M. Nixon's daughter, Julie Eisenhower, and other supporters broke ground for his presidential library in Yorba Linda, California. Ground was broken the first week of November 1989 for the Reagan Library. It has been reported in the newspaper that the $43 million cost will be picked up by private donations. The following are the eight libraries that are already in existence:

Herbert Hoover Presidential Library and Museum in West Branch, Iowa

Franklin D. Roosevelt Library in Hyde Park, New York

Harry S. Truman Library in Abilene, Kansas

Proper use of punctuation when listing libraries

Social Studies Fair Projects and Research Activities

4

John F. Kennedy Library in Boston, Massachusetts

Dwight D. Eisenhower Library in Abilene, Kansas

Lyndon B. Johnson Library & Museum in Austin, Texas

Gerald R. Ford Library in Grand Rapids, Michigan

Jimmy Carter Library in Atlanta, Georgia.

What can you expect to find in a Presidential Library? The most important documents are the White House files. These files cover all of the major issues of public policy. The papers of the Presidents constitute a very valuable part of our nation's history that cannot be understood or written about without these papers. These are the records created and received by the President and his staff, in the course of performing their official duties. These files cover all of the major issues of public policy.

Next, you can expect to find materials donated by individuals associated with the President during his term of office. These may be papers from people who held important positions in his administration, papers from his political party, or

Has Jon properly organized this paragraph?

5

papers from his family or papers from his personal friends.

A third group of materials consists of papers accumulated by the President prior to or following his presidential term. *Notice the proper use of an example.* For example, President Eisenhower's library has a section devoted to his military career. The Kennedy Library has materials relating to his years as a Congressman and a Senator.

Each library has a large collection of audio-visual materials. More and more materials are being computerized. In the Jimmy Carter Library, it was interesting how computers were used to program his answers to questions you could select to ask him.

Ideas closely follow the outline. Family heirlooms and items of personal interest are also found in the libraries. President Kennedy's favorite rocking chair can be found in his library. Some of Eisenhower's paintings are found in his library. In Roosevelt's library, you can see some of his favorite ship models.

Gifts given by individuals and foreign dignitaries are always displayed in the museum section of the library. Some

73

Social Studies Fair Projects and Research Activities

of these items may be handmade crafts given to a President. Some may be very expensive works of art.

We are fortunate to have the Jimmy Carter Presidential Library located here in Atlanta. As a part of my research for this paper I visited the library and found it to be very interesting. These libraries also serve the public by serving as a meeting place for conferences. They also sponsor lectures and films dealing with topics of historical or current interest.

Conclusion

Has Jon restated his thesis?

The purpose of a presidential library is to give visitors a better understanding of a particular President, of the office of the President, and the American political system. Each year teachers, students, and others come from all over to use the materials in the library for research purposes. A presidential library is unlike any other library. It is really more of a museum for people to walk through and leave knowing more about the man himself and our country during the years that he was president.

Bibliography

Notice *bibliography* is centered.

Jon has correctly alphabetized the bibliography.

Magazine article has been correctly listed.

Bibliography

Fenn, Dan H. Jr. "Launching the John F. Kennedy Library." The American Archivist. October,1979. Vol.42, No. 4, pp. 429-442.

Higgins, Jeff and Susan Wessling. "A President Remembered." New England: New England Newsclip Agency, Inc.

Kahn, Herman. "The Presidential Library- A New Institution." Franklin D. Roosevelt Library.

"Presidential Libraries: Where Tourists, Scholars Brush Elbows." U.S. News &World Report. July 11, 1977: pp.23-25.

Chapter Eleven

PREPARING THE BACKBOARD AND MODELS

How Do You Begin a Backboard?

1. It is extremely important to begin gathering materials for your backboard very early. Save everything: copies of every letter requesting information about the topic; magazine articles; newspaper articles; e-mails; photographs; pamphlets. Use a basket, drawer, or box to collect and save these items. Remember: Never throw anything away until the project is complete.

2. Buy or build the backboard. (The backboards may be purchased from most local office supply or school supply stores.) If you are making the backboard, purchase supplies from a local hardware store.

3. Backboards may be covered with fabric or paper, painted, or purchased in various colors.

4. Create a drawing of the backboard plan. Be sure to include the required parts of a backboard (see example on page 78). Try several sketches or plans so you can choose the one that best suits your purpose. Keep in mind that an orderly arrangement will bring unity to your work and that a preliminary sketch will help work problems out on paper.

5. If required, submit the final drawing to your teacher for approval.

6. Once approved, use the plan to lay out the letters and other items gathered on the backboard. Be sure to leave neat margins and good spacing for the letters.

7. Have someone check your lettering for correct spelling! Glue the letters and other documentation to the backboard.

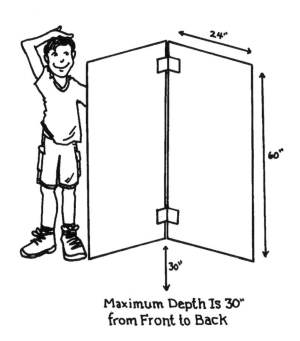

Maximum Depth Is 30"
from Front to Back

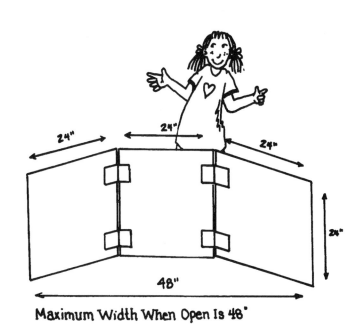

Maximum Width When Open Is 48"

Social Studies Fair Projects and Research Activities

What Type of Backboard Should be Used?

The backboard should be made of sturdy materials, such as plywood, pegboard, cardboard, or another material. Commercially prepared foam core or cardboard backboard (pre-folded for easy use), may be found at art, office, or school supply stores. The backboard should be no larger than 48" in width, 60" in height, and 30" in depth. See the illustration below for the correct use of a backboard.

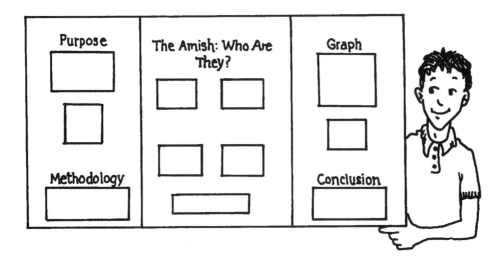

Advantages for Covering the Backboard

The color of the backboard may be part of the overall color scheme and may help reinforce the topic. A covered board should not fight the surface of the display board itself. For example, the grain of the wood, the texture of the circles in the pegboard, or the lines in the cardboard may compete with a design for attention. The background should be a part of the design and not something that works against it. Remember: A covered board should help bring unity to the display.

Materials for Covering the Backboard

Painting a backboard works well, especially if the backboard is made of plywood. If trying to paint cardboard, make sure the paint is not too thin or watery. Felt or fabric may also be used to cover the backboard, as long as the felt of fabric is not too thin. If you prefer, art craft paper may also be used to cover the backboard. A variety of colors is usually available. Finally, why not consider using a colorful border for the backboard? These borders are available in a wide variety of designs at local art, office, or school supply stores.

Social Studies Fair Projects and Research Activities

Decorating the Backboard

The materials for the backboard will depend on what is being illustrated. For example, use something as unusual as a fishing net if a topic calls for it. Try to be creative and use materials that will catch the eye of the audience and support the topic.

Design Elements

What design elements will make the backboard more attractive? An exceptional backboard is a work of art in itself. It reflects good composition and an orderly arrangement. The following principles of design will help to create good composition:

Center of Interest: Is there something that catches the eye? A center of interest draws a viewer's attention.

Color Scheme: The use of a color scheme will help to organize the backboard. The colors chosen may reflect the topic. For example, red, white, and blue for a political theme; pastels for a feminine issue; black and yellow for strong visual clarity; shades of blue for a marine topic; or black or white (with another color) to make a strong statement.

Contrast: Is there enough of a difference between the colors you have chosen to make for easy reading? The work should not fade into the background.

Balance: Check to see that the overall design is carried throughout the backboard. Try to make groups of items evenly distributed so that harmony is achieved.

Variety: Have you brought interest to your topic by using graphs, charts, maps, diagrams, timelines, or pictures?

Rhythm: An orderly progression is important to good composition. Since we read from left to right, it is advisable to place the *Purpose* on the left of the board and to end with the *Conclusion* on the right. Give the backboard a well-thought out sense of order; it will be more easily understood and read by the viewer.

Unity: This principle of design shows oneness. Ask yourself: Does my backboard work with all the parts coming together as a whole? A backboard will achieve unity if all the parts are necessary. Do not overdo your project! Make your work clear and concise. *

*Adapted from DeKalb County School System's *Social Studies Project Handbook.*

Social Studies Fair Projects and Research Activities

Types of Lettering

Lettering is important in communicating the topic and research. The title should be bold with large lettering to clearly state the purpose of the social studies project. Lettering should be consistent. In other words, keep your letters the same size in each section. The lettering should be even. Uphill or downhill lettering draws the eye like a magnet! Take time to measure the letters so that the right distance is left between letters and words. Do not allow the letters to run off the edges of the backboard.

Lettering Possibilities:

- Letters cut from felt or construction paper (free-hand or die-cut)

- Neatly drawn letters colored in with markers

- Punch-out letters, such as cardboard, vinyl, or plastic

- Stenciled letters, available in various sizes

- Computerized lettering, available in a variety of fonts

- Lettering printed on strips of clear tape (special machine needed)

Parts of the Backboard

Each backboard must have the following information:

1. A 3 x 5 card attached to the front of the backboard, which has the class (grade level), discipline under which each project will be judged, name of the student, name of the supervising teacher, and name of the school

2. **Title** of the project (in the form of a question)

3. **Purpose** of the project (the thesis and the introduction)

4. **Methodology** used for researching or investigating the topic

5. Visuals to illustrate the topic (pictures, charts, graphs, maps, etc.)

6. **Conclusion** to the question researched (may be taken directly from the conclusion in the body of the research paper)*

*Adapted from DeKalb County School System's *Social Studies Project Handbook.*

Avoiding Backboard Pitfalls

1. Avoid using white-out because it draws the viewer's eyes to the mistake.

2. Use spray fixatives in a well-vented area. White glue will wrinkle the paper and has "no give" for re-positioning letters or pictures after it is used.

3. Use straight pins to place materials prior to gluing. Items can still be rearranged, yet it will avoid unwanted movement.

4. Pin a piece of yarn at equal distances from the top of the backboard to use as a guideline for placing letters. Use a kneaded eraser to clean up drawn guidelines. Kneaded erasers will not leave a smear.

5. Take time to cut out pictures and graphs evenly. Ragged edges will draw attention.

6. For a framed look, use construction paper or colored paper to mat your pictures and graphs.

7. Use a handmade or purchased decorative border of some kind.

8. Rubber cement is a terrific adhesive, but it must be used in a vented area. If some of the rubber cement shows on the front of the backboard, just let it dry and rub it into little balls for easy cleanup.

9. Never mark on uncovered foam-board. It is possible to erase the lead marking, but it will leave an impression.

Social Studies Fair Projects and Research Activities

Rules Concerning Audio-Visuals

Audio-visual materials may be used to coordinate with a topic. Some examples of the types of audio-visual equipment are slide shows, taped interviews, video presentations, and Powerpoint presentations.

Student Responsibility

Any audio-visual equipment that is needed for the student's presentation must be furnished by the student. Generally speaking, school equipment is not loaned to the student for such purposes. Also, it is the student's responsibility to furnish extension cords and to see that these cords do not cause a safety hazard.

Equipment Security

It is the responsibility of the student to protect all audio-visual equipment from theft. It is recommended that monitors, VCR's, cassette players, and any other audio-visual equipment be secured or chained to the table.

Audio-Visual Time Limit

Normally speaking, presentations should not exceed ten (10) minutes total time.

Social Studies Fair Projects and Research Activities

Model Types

Models can enhance a social studies project by giving a three-dimensional interpretation of the topic. Some examples of models or display items to include as part of a project are as follows:

Dioramas	Maps	Photographs
Artifacts	Films	Filmstrips
Charts	Murals	Video Tapes
Diagrams	Recordings	Slides
Historical Collections	Graphs	Models

Model Rules

Any object or item that can be made by the student should be made by the student. The use of commercial models, such as model planes and ships, toy soldiers, toy furniture or dishes, and any other commercial objects is prohibited.

Model Material

Modeling clay, wood, plaster, papier mâché, pipe cleaners, tooth picks, craft sticks, paper clay (does not have to be fired), styrofoam, cardboard, paper tubes, fabric (including felt), construction paper, boxes, tissue paper, and aluminum foil may be used.

Objects of Value

Students are encouraged to make replicas, if possible, instead of using valuable collections. For example, make an arrowhead collection from plaster rather than displaying the real thing. Security is an area of concern; therefore, students are asked to avoid displaying valuable items.

Social Studies Fair Projects and Research Activities

Chapter Twelve

BACKBOARD PROJECT EXAMPLES

History Project Example

The following is an example of a Social Studies History Project:

Project Analysis

Question: What Characterized The Shaker Society?

Backboard: Black along the bottom only

Border: None

Mats: Photographs, labels, and writings are matted on black construction paper.

Labels: Purpose, Methodology, Conclusion

Social Studies Fair Projects and Research Activities

Geography Project Example

The following is an example of a Social Studies Geography Project:

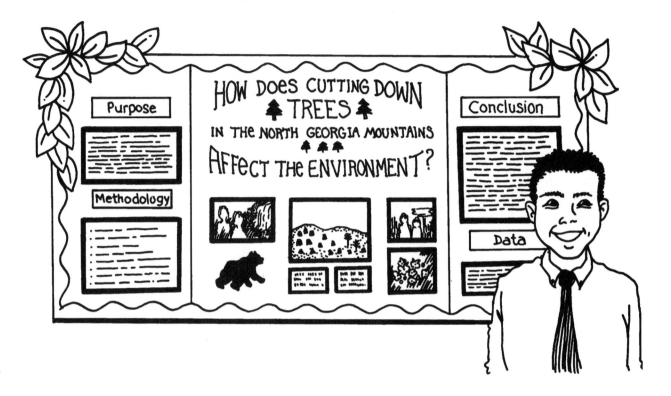

Project Analysis

Question: How Does Cutting Down Trees in the North Georgia Mountains Affect the Environment?

Backboard: White

Border: Green scalloped border and green leaves

Mats: Photos, labels, and all written work are matted on black construction paper.

Labels: Purpose, Methodology, Conclusion, Data

Social Studies Fair Projects and Research Activities — Copyright ©2001 by Incentive Publications, Inc., Nashville, TN.

Political Science Project Example

The following is an example of a Social Studies Political Science Project:

Project Analysis

Question: Hillary: Presidential Wife or Policy Maker?

Backboard: Red

Border: Red, white, and blue stars

Mats: Photos, labels, and all written work are matted on blue construction paper.

Labels: Purpose, Methodology, Data, Graphs, Conclusion

Social Studies Fair Projects and Research Activities

Economics Project Example

The following is an example of a Social Studies Economics Project:

Project Analysis

Question: Investing in Stocks: Do the Rewards Outweigh the Risks?

Backboard: White

Lettering: Black

Border: Green scalloped border with play money glued on top

Model: Balance scale made from wood, painted black with objects wrapped with paper and labeled as Risks and Rewards.

Mats: Green construction paper used for matting behind graphs, conclusion, purpose, methodology and data.

Labels: Purpose, Data, Methodology, Statistics, Conclusion

Anthropology Project Example

The following is an example of a Social Studies Anthropology Project:

Project Analysis

Question: Ancient Egyptian Mummification: What Were the Procedures and Rituals?

Backboard: Black

Border: Hieroglyphic pictures down the sides

Mats: Orange construction paper is used to mat the pictures, label, and writing.

Labels: Methodology, Data, Purpose, Conclusion

Social Studies Fair Projects and Research Activities

Sociology Project Example

The following is an example of a Social Studies Sociology Project:

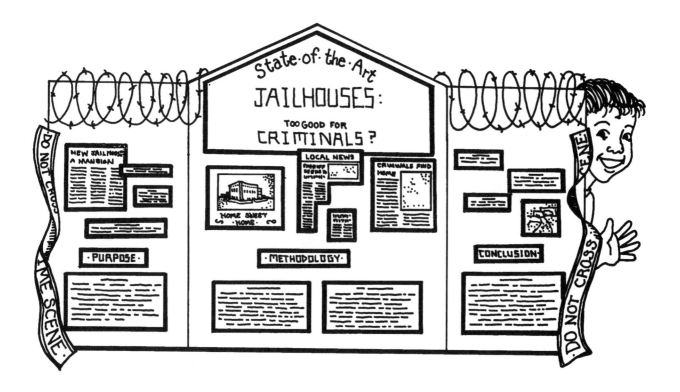

Project Analysis

Question: State of the Art Jailhouses: Too Good for Criminals?

Backboard: White

Lettering: Black on yellow paper

Border: Yellow and black crime scene tape on left and right sides, coil of barbed wire across top

Mats: Pictures, news articles, and photos are matted on black construction paper. Conclusion, methodology, and purpose written on yellow paper and matted on black construction paper.

Labels: Purpose, Methodology, Conclusion

APPENDIX

Date: _____

Dear Parent:

Preparations for the annual (school name) Social Studies Fair are in progress. Today your child received information which outlines the requirements, format, and due dates for the project. If he/she intends to participate in the Social Studies Fair, a research paper and an accompanying backboard are required.

Please review this information with your child today, just as we have done at school. Your child will need help and support in choosing a topic and locating information. However, a successful project for your child will represent his/her work, not that of a parent or expert.

This project will provide a variety of educational experiences. Students will take notes, make an outline, write a thesis statement, write a research paper, and organize a bibliography. Students who prepare a backboard will gain artistic skills in lettering, spacing, and balance. Classroom teachers are also working with your child to help him/her develop these skills.

Please be aware of the calendar and help your child plan assignments in accordance with the due dates for each aspect of the project. A pocket folder is ideal for organizing all information and research. Note cards are suggested for taking notes. Prior to submitting the rough draft, your child will ask you to proofread his/her paper for grammar and spelling errors.

Your cooperation and support are appreciated in this valuable learning experience. After reviewing this information with your child, please sign the bottom portion of this letter and return it.

Sincerely,

- -

Dear _____,

I have reviewed the Social Studies Fair Project information with my child, _____ (child's name).

_____   _____
Date   Parent/Guardian Signature

Tips for Parents/Guardians*

1. Go over all information regarding the social studies project with your child. If you have any questions, contact the teacher who distributed the information.

2. Help your child choose a topic and be supportive of his/her final decision.

3. Allow your child time for thinking, exploring, and preparing his/her project.

4. Help your child by doing the following:

   a) driving him/her to the library

   b) helping to arrange interviews

   c) providing suggestions as to sources of information

   d) helping to create and compile surveys

   e) proofreading and revising letters requesting information and/or materials

   f) gathering printed materials related to your child's project

   g) making suggestions for backboard design improvement

   h) assisting in model construction

   > **Remember:** You are to _assist_ your child in the completion of his/her social studies project. The operative word is _assist_. If the social studies project is to be a true learning experience for your child, it is imperative that the work be completed _by the child_.

5. Proofread all material for grammatical correctness and content.

6. Be aware that your child may need assistance in delivering the project to and from school.

7. Show your support by going to your school, city, or county social studies fair with your child.

*Adapted from DeKalb County School System's _Social Studies Fair Handbook_.

Social Studies Fair Projects and Research Activities

Date _____

Dear Student:

Today you are receiving Social Studies Fair information which outlines requirements, format, and due dates. If you intend to participate in the _____ (name of school) Social Studies Fair, a research paper and accompanying backboard are required. Your research paper will be included in your Social Studies grade.

Please review the information in this packet with your parents. You may need help and support choosing a topic and locating information. Remember that parents need advance notice and reminders when you must be driven somewhere, so ask first and give some lead time. A successful project will represent your own work—not that of a parent or expert. A pocket folder is ideal for organizing and keeping all project information and research. Note cards are necessary for taking notes.

The final research paper will be **2–4 typewritten pages** or **3–8 handwritten pages** in length, using a variety of resources, with no more than one encyclopedia as a source. Before turning in your rough draft, ask your parents or an adult to proofread your paper for grammar and spelling errors.

The project will help you develop many of the skills necessary for a successful academic and business career. Doing research, compiling notes, making a good working outline, writing a well-planned and documented paper, and creating a visual display that you are proud of will develop organizational skills and give you confidence.

Please be aware of the calendar and plan your work assignments according to the due dates for each aspect of the project. Enthusiasm and motivation are essential for a successful project. Remember, choose a topic that you really like, and have fun rising to the challenge .

Sincerely,

DECISION MAKING:
TOPIC FOR RESEARCH PROJECT

1. Listed below are some of MY CHOICES for my Social Studies Research Project:

   _____

   _____

   _____

2. Using the choices above, ask yourself the following questions to assist you in making a decision. Develop a code by which you weigh the answers for each question. (For example: Yes, No, or Maybe). Use these answers to help make your decision of which choice to pursue.

   A. Is this a topic that is exciting to me?

   B. Besides the encyclopedia, are there at least 2 other sources of information?

   C. Does this topic relate to one of the 6 Disciplines of Social Studies?

   D. Will I be able to easily present this topic with a visual display?

   E. Is there too much information on this topic?

3. MY SOCIAL STUDIES PROJECT TOPIC IS _____.

4. My varied reasons for my choice are: (Note: Your reasons must relate to the criteria established in #2.)

   A. _____

   B. _____

   C. _____

   D. _____

   E. _____

   F. _____

Student's Signature: _____ Date: _____

Parent's Signature: _____ Date: _____

Social Studies Fair Projects and Research Activities

Research Proposal Sheet

Student's Name: _____   Teacher: _____

SECTION I:

Question: _____

_____

Social Studies Discipline: _____

Teacher Suggestions: _____

_____

SECTION II:

Rewritten Question: _____

_____

Social Studies Discipline: _____

SECTION III:

What resources do you plan to use to answer your question? (You must name at least 3 different sources, using only one encyclopedia.)

1. _____

2. _____

3. _____

Teacher Suggestions: _____

_____

_____

_____

Parent's Signature: _____   Date: _____

Social Studies Project Rubric

Student Name _____

Project Title _____

	Excellent (4)	Good (3)	Fair (2)	Unsatisfactory (1)
Scale I: Knowledge	1. Demonstrates a thorough, accurate, and coherent explanation of the topic.	1. Demonstrates a fairly thorough and reasonably accurate explanation of the topic.	1. Partial explanation of topic given with some major elements that are missing.	1. No explanation of topic.
	2. Clearly identifies question researched for the project.	2. Adequately identifies question researched for the project.	2. Question researched is not identified correctly.	2. Question researched is not presented appropriately.
	3. Appropriate and relevant facts are gathered and well organized.	3. Facts are adequate but minimal.	3. Facts are present but muddled and unorganized.	3. Basic information is inadequate.
Scale II: Quality of Presentation	1. The exhibit is creative and effectively addresses the question researched in a clear and concise manner.	1. The exhibit is interesting and adequately addresses the question researched.	1. The exhibit shows vague references to the question that has been researched.	1. The exhibit is not related to the question researched.
	2. Project flows logically from beginning to end.	2. The project adequately flows from beginning to end.	2. The project is unclear and is missing vital elements.	2. Overall project lacks clarity.
	3. Physical appearance of the project shows attention to detail in terms of lettering, organization, typing, proofreading, neatness, etc.	3. Good physical appearance.	3. Major errors in attention to detail.	3. Gross errors in attention to detail.
		4. Minor flaws in terms of typing, neatness, proofreading, etc.		

*Adapted from Chicago Public Schools Bureau of Student Assessment.

Social Studies Project Rubric

Student Name _____   Project Title _____

	Excellent (4)	Good (3)	Fair (2)	Unsatisfactory (1)
Scale III: Quality of Analysis	1. Clearly tells a story of change over time. 2. Effectively deals with a problem or question and proceeds to resolve or answer it. 3. Formulates a conclusion statement. 4. Strong supportive arguments are used. 5. Resolutions are persuasive and based on research.	1. Tells a story of change over time. 2. Addresses problem and resolves them. 3. Supportive arguments are somewhat clear and organized. 4. Resolutions are fairly persuasive.	1. Insufficiently tells the story of change over time. 2. Project barely addresses problems. 3. Arguments are vague and unclear. 4. Shows little evidence of resolution of problem.	1. Project fails to tell story of change over time. 2. Project does not address problems. 3. Arguments are not supported. 4. Problems are not resolved.
Scale IV: Quality of Sources	1. Bibliography includes exceptional sources. 2. Sources consulted include several institutions. 3. Bibliography includes a wide variety of primary and secondary sources. 4. Bibliography is in alphabetical order. 5. Citations are in correct format.	1. Bibliography includes sufficient sources. 2. Sources consulted include one or two institutions. 3. Bibliography includes a sufficient number of primary and/or secondary sources. 4. Bibliography is in alphabetical order.	1. Bibliography lacks sufficient sources. 2. Sources consulted included at least one institution.	Bibliography is inaccurate or missing.

*Adapted from Chicago Public Schools Bureau of Student Assessment.

Suggested Roles of Responsibility

The successful completion of the Social Studies Project requires much support and assistance. It is strongly advised that all faculty and staff members provide support to those teachers primarily responsible for the projects. Listed below are some recommendations for involvement of the entire staff.

Principal and Administrators

- Select date for local Social Studies Fair
- Appoint a committee to plan and coordinate local fair
- Provide certificates for all participants in the fair

Media Specialist

- Serve as resource teacher for the research process
- Assist students in identifying appropriate resource material
- Work with teachers to schedule research time in the media center

Computer Specialist

- Assist students in the proper use of computer equipment
- Help students with appropriate word processing software

Faculty/Staff

- Help students select topics
- Cut out letters
- Help students obtain research material
- Check first draft and make suggestions for revisions
- Proofread the research paper
- Help with backboard design
- Provide encouragement and praise

Custodians

- Help with the setup of areas that will be used for project viewing by parents, faculty, staff, and students

Judge's Score Sheet

CIRCLE ONE:
Excellent = 90–100
Good = 80–89
Fair = 70–79

Table _____

Place _____

SCHOOL _____

STUDENT'S NAME _____

TITLE OF PROJECT _____

DISCIPLINE _____ CLASS _____

Note: Judges are requested to use the following criteria in judging all projects on all grade levels at local, regional, and state fairs. **Circle the letters of the areas that need improving.**

I. METHODOLOGY - DEVELOPMENT OF THE TOPIC (60 POINTS)

The project demonstrates:

A. clarity of objective

B. analysis (broken down into its component parts, which includes purpose and/or hypothesis, methodology, conclusion)

C. adequacy of methodology (adequate and reliable sources: sufficient data to support conclusions)

D. evidence of critical thinking (evaluation and interpretation of data)

E. appropriate social studies skills (e.g., gathering and interpreting data, time and chronology, maps, and globes)

F. appropriateness of topic (neither too limited nor too broad)

G. relevance (all information shown is directly related to the project idea)

H. an important aspect of human experience

I. (approximately 2–4 typewritten or 3–8 handwritten pages) a summary of the research that includes purpose, development, and interpretation of the idea and conclusion

J. correct grammar, spelling, punctuation, and bibliographic style

II. EFFECTIVENESS OF PRESENTATION (40 POINTS)

The project demonstrates:

A. appropriate choice of media or format for presentation of data

B. clarity in presentation

C. good organization

D. conscientiousness of effort as manifested by (a) accuracy, (b) neatness, (c) craftsmanship

E. a pleasing visual and/or auditory effect

F. a backboard within size limitations, including a statement of purpose, procedures, conclusion, and data that is arranged in a clear and meaningful manner

G. creativity or originality in construction, arrangement, or presentation of material

TOTAL SCORE: _____

CRITIQUE _____

_____

_____

Social Studies Fair Projects and Research Activities   Copyright ©2001 by Incentive Publications, Inc., Nashville, TN.

CHECKLIST FOR THE COMPLETED PROJECT

	YES	NO
1. Is my research question appropriately stated?		
2. Is my written report clear, concise, and grammatically correct?		
3. Are all words spelled correctly?		
4. Does my written report include:		
a. Title page		
b. Verification page (Include only if someone else typed your paper)		
c. Purpose page		
d. Methodology page		
e. Research		
f. Conclusion page		
g. Bibliography		
h. Credit page (Optional: Use this page to give recognition to someone who was especially helpful to you.)		
5. Is my exhibit durable and easily movable?		
6. Is my exhibit appropriate for the particular discipline?		
7. Does my backboard include:		
a. A clear statement of the question researched		
b. Purpose		
c. Methodology		
d. Evidence of my research		
e. Conclusion		
8. Is my name and other required information included on both my written report and my display?		
9. Have I set up my completed report and done a final examination of my entire display?		
10. Is my exhibit attractive and appealing?		
11. Have I gained knowledge as a result of doing this project?		

101

SOCIAL STUDIES PROJECT: BEST WEB SITES

The American Experience

http://www.pbs.org/wgbh/amex/highlights.html

Since 1988, PBS has broadcast The American Experience, a splendid, award-winning, historical documentary series produced by WBGH. The series has featured outstanding biographies of the noble and notorious, gripping stories of natural disasters, the tragedies of wartime, and the challenges faced by a diverse population. News of upcoming programs can be found on the Web page.

[WBGH; Public Broadcasting System]

American History Archive Project

http://www.ilt.columbia.edu/k12/history/aha.html

This well-organized archive of Web links to American history resources includes interesting samples of student Web page history projects. These can serve as useful American history models.

[Institute for Learning Technologies]

American History: The History Net Archives

http://www.thehistorynet.com/THNarchives/AmericanHistory

This megasite overflows with excellent content, superbly written articles, and beautiful color images. Unlike most archives, which are merely collections of links to other sites, the History Net contains a large archive of original items. Just a small sample of the articles contained in the archives:
- 1797: The First Real Election
- Blue Ridge Traditions
- Civil War Railroads
- The Death and Life of Stonewall Jackson
- Life in Early America: The Worst Winters
- Personality: Henry Ford
- Undercover: German Saboteurs in America

[American History Society]

Anatomy of a Murder: A Trip Through Our Nation's Legal Justice System

http://tqd.advanced.org/2760/

A winner in the ThinkQuest '96 student competition, this splendid tutorial guides users through the maze of the legal justice system as they follow a murder suspect from arrest through trial. This well-researched multimedia lesson will hold the attention of all learners. The legal nuances of the criminal prosecution of accused murders are detailed in clear and accurate language. A hypertext glossary helps with the legal terms. What a great learning experience!

[Michael Morley, Chris Stiner, and Michael Hammer; Cranford High School, Cranford, NJ]

History Channel

http://www.historychannel.com/index2.html

A rich resource of tips, activities, study guides, and classroom materials to accompany cable television's outstanding History Channel programs. You have permission to videotape the History Channel programs and use them for up to one year. Past programs may also be purchased rather inexpensively. "This Day in History" provides searchable database of noted historical events which occurred on each day of the year. For teachers, you can post the day's historical anniversaries on the bulletin board or on an overhead as a great interest-arousing feature for history classes.

History Net

http://www.thehistorynet.com/

This top-notch megasite, a history buff's view of paradise, is filled with material on all aspects of world and American history. The "Today in History" section features dozens of historical events which occurred on each day of the year. The "History Net Archives" is stocked with a multitude of fascinating links.

[American Historical Society]

Historical Maps of the United States

http:www.lib.utexas.edu/Libs/PCL/Map_collection/histus.html

An on-line collection of historical maps records the territorial growth, distribution of early Indian tribes, exploration, and settlement of the United States.

[The Perry-Castarieda Library Map Collection, The University of Texas at Austin]

Historical Text Archive

http://www.geocities.com/djmabry/index.html

The creator of this site has done a great service for students, teachers, and historians by assembling digitized versions of numerous primary documents and texts related to world history. The documents are arranged by geographical region as well as by topic.

[Don Mabry, Mississippi State University]

The HistoryNet: World History

http://www.thehistorynet.com/THNarchives/WorldHistory/

Bookmark this site. It is a winner, filled with well-researched, articulate articles covering a wide range of world history topics. The frequently updated site includes special interviews, eyewitness accounts, personality profiles, noteworthy battles, historic travels, and book reviews.

National Election Studies

http://www.umich.edu/~nes/nesguide/nesguide.htm

The N.E.S. Guide to Public Opinion and Electoral Behavior provides instant access to tables and graphs of public opinion and election results since 1952. Among the data displays are the following: Support for the Political System; Evaluation of the Presidential Candidates; Public Opinion on Public Policy Issues; and Evaluation of Congressional Candidates.

[U.S. National Science Foundation funded; Center for Political Studies at the University of Michigan's Institute for Social Research]

In recognition of an outstanding Social Studies Project

_____

is hereby awarded this

Certificate of Achievement

Presented on this _____ day of _____, 20_____

_____   _____
Signature   Signature

Social Studies Fair Projects and Research Activities

Answer Key

Finding a Good Topic to Research

Teachers sometimes assign topics for students to research in the library. At other times, students can choose topics on their own. If a teacher asks students to choose a topic, students will need to know how to avoid choosing the wrong one. There are at least five kinds of poor topic choices. The following difficulties should be considered before students look for information in the library:

1. **Some topics are too small.**
   Example: What do you know about your ancestors?
   A student cannot write a research paper on a topic that can be explained in one or two sentences.

2. **Some topics are too big.**
   Example: What are the different holidays?
   Topics which are too big make it impossible for us to find all the information that is necessary to cover the topic adequately.

3. **Some topics simply have no information available.**
   Example: Why did Christopher Columbus quarrel with his shipmates?
   We do not know why people behave in a certain manner.

4. **Some topics are confusing because we cannot tell exactly what information is requested.**
   Example: What do teenagers like?
   We know that teenagers have different likes and dislikes.

5. **Some topics concern questions in which people throughout the world cannot agree.**
   Example: What was the world's best invention?
   People have different opinions, and therefore, cannot agree.

Can you now recall the five problems listed above without looking? List them below.

1. *too small*
2. *too big*
3. *no information available*
4. *confusing*
5. *people cannot agree*

Recognizing Poor Topics

The topics below are poor choices for a social studies research paper because of the previously discussed reasons. On the line beneath each topic, write the reason or reasons why it should not be chosen.

1. What country has the most beautiful scenery in the world?
   people cannot agree

2. How have people built their cities since early times?
   too big

3. What would be the best way to improve things?
   too big; confusing

4. What kind of government does Russia have?
   too small

5. When did Pizarro make his first trip to Latin America?
   too small

6. Why did Alexander the Great like horses?
   no information available; too small

7. What kinds of weapons have been used by people since early times?
   too big

8. How tall is the Statue of Liberty?
   too small

- **Copy:** Write or type the report as neatly as possible.
- Make the cover attractive so that it will coordinate with the entire project.
- Create a bibliography.
- **Check:** Reread the report to make sure no important information has been left out and no mistakes were made in copying.*

Adapted from the DeKalb County School System's Social Studies Fair Handbook, Decatur, GA.

Proofreading Activity

While writing a research paper, it always helps to proofread, or "proof" what has been written. When proofreading, make sure the punctuation, capitalization, and spelling are correct.

Read the paragraph below. The paragraph has mistakes in punctuation, capitalization, and spelling. First, draw a circle around each mistake. Then, in the space provided, rewrite the paragraph correcting all mistakes. THERE ARE 10 MISTAKES. Can you find all of them?

the origin of furniture as we know it goes back to ancient Egypt. The Egyptians had stools chairs chests tables and beds; examples of which can be seen in museums today. They put such everyday objects in the Tombs. They also painted scenes of every day life on the walls of the tombs. Some of these were indoor scenes that showed an abundence of furniture. Many century later, when the sealed tombs were opened examples of both the real furniture and the furniture painted on the walls were found.**

The origin of furniture as we know it goes back to ancient Egypt. The Egyptians had stools, chairs, chests, tables, and beds; examples of which can be seen in museums today. They put such everyday objects in the tombs. They also painted scenes of everyday life on the walls of the tombs. Some of these were indoor scenes that showed an abundance of furniture. Many centuries later, when the sealed tombs were opened, examples of both the real furniture and the furniture painted on the walls were found.

**Adapted from Building Proofreading Skills, Incentive Publications, Nashville, TN.*

Practice Note Taking

Use your judgment in choosing the most important and least important statements. Read the article carefully and then answer the questions that follow.

Benjamin Franklin, An Extraordinary Man

Benjamin Franklin, one of the most extraordinary men in American history, was the fifteenth child in a family of seventeen children. Because Benjamin's father was a candle maker, Benjamin had to drop out of school very early to help his father in his work; however, this did not keep his mind from stretching in many directions.

Benjamin did so many interesting things that it is difficult to list them all. After studying electricity, he invented the lightning rod. He also invented bifocal glasses that allowed people to see both near and far. The Franklin stove, another of his inventions, made the heating of homes much more efficient and economical. In addition to showing farmers how to improve acidic soil by using lime, he also taught sailors how to calm stormy seas by pouring oil on the surface of the water.

Franklin served his country in many ways. As assistant to the Postmaster General of the Colonies, he organized the first postal delivery system. As Minister to France, he helped greatly in winning the Revolutionary War. He also did much to assure the success of the Constitutional Convention by offering the compromise amendment which prevented the break-up of the new governing body.

As a writer and educator, Franklin developed and published the *Pennsylvania Gazette* which carried the first cartoons and maps ever printed in newspapers. His interest in education led him to start an academy which offered high school studies. This school later developed into the University of Pennsylvania.

Which two contributions were the two most important to the establishment of our country?

1. *assistant to the Postmaster General - postal delivery*
2. *offered compromise amendment at Constitutional Convention*

Which two accomplishments were the least important to the establishment of our country?

1. *invented lightning rod*
2. *invented Franklin stove*

Which contribution by Franklin was the most important to people's health?

invention of bifocal lenses

Practice Note Taking

When taking notes, begin by skimming the material in order to get a general idea of the content. When reading the material for the second time, read more carefully in order to find the main points and details. Instead of writing complete sentences, make brief notes.

On the right side of this page, take notes on the article below. Remember to use brief notes instead of complete sentences. Check the article for main ideas, cue words, and punctuation. Remember to use quotation marks for direct quotes.

Uruguay	Your Notes
Uruguay, one of the smallest of the South American republics, is located on the east coast of the continent between Brazil and Argentina. A land of gently rolling hills and temperate climate, it is the only South American country with no large uninhabited areas.	-Uruguay - one of smallest republics in S.A. -location - between Brazil and Argentina - on E. coast -land - gently rolling hills -climate - mild
At first, most of Uruguay's settlers came from Spain. People later arrived from many other countries. In the mid 1800's, there was an influx of British settlers. Blacks immigrated to Uruguay from Brazil soon after Brazil abolished slavery. Other Europeans have also settled in Uruguay.	-population - evenly distributed Settlers - 1st Spanish 1800's - British blacks from Brazil others from Europe
Uruguay is one of the smallest and most unified countries in South America, but its people follow two distinct ways of life: rural and urban. The rural life is typified by the gauchos—the colorful cattle or sheep herders of the region. Urban life in Uruguay is similar to that found in Europe. Careful appearance and behavior, good manners, and a love of culture are important to their way of life.	Uruguay - one of smallest in S.A. - most unified in S.A. two ways of life - 1) rural 2) urban rural - cowboys (gauchos) urban - like Europe important: ① look good ② good behavior ③ good manners ④ love culture

Practice Outlining

Read the story below and then fill in the outline under the major headings.

The Growth of the Roman Empire

Nearly 3,000 years ago, ancient people were tending their simple farms in a region of Italy that later became a part of Rome. Rome, in turn, became the center of the Roman Empire. These early people began trading in one of the valleys between the seven hills where the city of Rome gradually developed. This valley between the hills became known as the market place, or forum.

As Rome grew, the Romans took over more land. They conquered tribes nearby and then built walls to protect the lands they had conquered. One of the early kings, Servius, built a wall entirely around the city to keep enemies out. The Romans were able to conquer many different tribes of people because they were able to work together very well. They were proud of their accomplishments.

The Romans sent armies south to conquer the southern part of Italy. Gradually these same armies made their way across the Mediterranean Sea to Africa where they conquered the great city of Carthage. The land in Africa was ideal for growing wheat. It was not long before Roman ships were sailing back and forth across the Mediterranean Sea, carrying wheat from North Africa to feed the people of Rome. The Romans conquered lands at the eastern and western ends of the Mediterranean Sea as well.

The Romans were great builders. They constructed pipelines known as aqueducts to carry fresh water into their cities, and they built stone roads and bridges to help in the movement of goods and armies from one part of the empire to another. The Romans also constructed huge walls to protect their boundaries. Many of these aqueducts, roads, bridges, and walls can be seen today. In Rome itself, the Romans built beautiful temples, stadiums, and other public buildings. Thousands of people go to Rome each year to see the remains of these great buildings.*

I. The Founding of Rome

  A. 3,000 years ago farmers began tending

  B. valley between hills known as forum

II. Changes That Took Place as Rome Grew

  A. Romans took more land

  B. built a wall to keep enemies out

III. Roman Accomplishments in Building

  A. aqueducts, pipelines to carry fresh water

  B. stone roads and bridges

  C. beautiful temples, stadiums, and public buildings

*Adapted from DeKalb County School System's Social Studies Fair Handbook, Decatur, GA.

Further Outline Practice

To further test your knowledge of outlines, parts of two outlines are given below. The outlines are in scrambled order. For the first outline, the form is supplied for you. For the second outline, you are on your own.

	Scotland

Government
English
Homes
Language
Episcopalian
Manufacturing
People
Baptist
Economy
Gaelic
Natural Resources
Church of Scotland
Lifestyles
Agriculture
Recreation
Religion
	I. Government
	II. People
	  A. Language
	    1. English
	    2. Gaelic
	  B. Lifestyles
	    1. Homes
	    2. Recreation
	  C. Religion
	    1. Church of Scotland
	    2. Baptist
	    3. Episcopalian
	III. Economy
	  A. Natural Resources
	  B. Manufacturing
	  C. Agriculture

Suggestion: It might be wise to put in the Roman numerals first for each of the two main topics and leave space for the subtopics under each main topic.

	Chester A. Arthur

Boyhood
Political Growth
Early Life
Election
Legal Career
Family
Opposition
Political and Public Career
	I. Early Life
	  A. Boyhood
	  B. Family
	II. Political and Public Career
	  A. Political Growth
	  B. Legal Career
	  C. Opposition
	  D. Election

Practice Writing a Thesis Statement

Complete the following by writing a thesis statement for each question.

1. Question: Can we save the ozone layer from destruction?

Thesis: The ozone layer should be saved in order to protect people from skin cancer and to save the food chain.

2. Question: Should women be drafted in the armed services?

Thesis: If women want true equality they should be drafted in the armed services.

3. Question: What can be done about teenage pregnancies?

Thesis: The number of teenage pregnancies can be reduced by improving sex education in our schools.

4. Question: The Nile River: Why is it considered a cradle of civilization?

Thesis: One of the earliest and most advanced civilizations began near the Nile River; therefore, it is considered a cradle of civilization.

5. Question: Shoplifting: Is it really worth it?

Thesis: The penalties for shoplifting outweigh the thrills.

6. Question: Did humankind originate in Africa?

Thesis: According to scientific research, humankind did originate in Africa.

Practice Rewriting the Introductory Paragraph

While writing the introductory paragraph, please keep in mind that it is important to state the reason(s) for choosing this topic and to explain what will be proven in the research paper.

Directions: Edit the following first draft paragraph. While rewriting the paragraph, feel free to change any of the words, place the sentences in a more logical order, and remove any sentences that do not agree with the main topic. Also, correct any errors in spelling, capitalization, and punctuation.

I also wanted to know if my personality fits in with my birth order. This topic was chosen because I have always been intersted in birth order and personality. In this report, I will discuss what many studies prove about birth order and what many psychologists think about birth order. Does birth order determine personality? Only children are the only children that parents give birth to. I will try to determine how well previous findings predict ones personality and also try to discover new personality traits that follow the order of one's birth.

I have always been interested in birth order and personality. I also wanted to know if my personality fits in with my birth order. In this report, I will discuss what many studies prove about birth order and what many psychologists think about birth order. I will try to determine how well previous findings predict one's personality and also try to discover new personality traits that follow the order of one's birth.

Practice Rewriting a Conclusion

Remember that the concluding paragraph(s) should restate the thesis and should include any opinions of the writer based on the research and study described in the report.

Read the following conclusion. Feel free to change any of the words, place the sentences in a more logical order, and remove any sentences that do not agree with the main topic. Also, correct any errors in spelling, capitalization, and punctuation.

It is really more a museum for people to walk through and leave knowing more about the man and our country during the years that he was president. The purpose of a Presidential Library is to give visitors to the library a better understanding of the particular president, of the office of the President, and the American political system. Each year teachers, students, and others come from all over the country to use the materials in the library for research purposes. The Presidential Records Act of 1978 made it a requirement for presidents to donate official papers to the government. A presidential library is unlike any other library.

A presidential library is unlike any other library. The purpose of a Presidential Library is to give visitors to the library a better understanding of the particular president, the office of the President, and the American political system. It is really more a museum for people to walk through and leave knowing more about the man and our country during the years that he was president. Each year teachers, students, and others come from all over the country to use the materials in the library for research purposes.

Writing the Thesis Statement and Introductory Paragraph

In the space provided, write a thesis statement and an introductory paragraph. Continue writing the first draft on notebook paper.

Answers will vary.
Title of Research Paper

Thesis Statement: _Answers will vary._

Introductory Paragraph: _Answers will vary._

Writing the Conclusion

In the space provided, write your conclusion. Remember that the conclusion can be one or two paragraphs. It should restate the thesis and include any opinions that support the thesis.

Answers will vary.

Writing Bibliographical Entries

When writing a research paper, it is necessary to include a bibliography at the end. The bibliography is a list of all the sources used when gathering information for the paper. Bibliographies follow a special format and list important information about the sources. Write bibliographical entries for the sources listed below. Use the example as a guide.

Example: "Presidential Libraries: Where Tourists, Scholars Brush Elbows." <u>U.S. News & World Report</u>. July 11, 1977, pp. 23–25.

1. A book called The Life and Times of Judge Judy was written by John Law Your and published by Jurisprudence Publishers, New York, in 1999.

    Your, John Law. The Life and Times of Judge Judy. New York: Jurisprudence Publishers, 1999.

2. Army Ants was an article written by Clark Roach for the Orkin Encyclopedia, Vol. A, and published in 1998.

    Roach, Clark. "Army Ants." Orkin Encyclopedia. Vol. A, 1998.

3. A book called Worms—Love 'Em or Leave 'Em was written by Rigg Lee and published by Pete Moss Publishers, New York, in 1982.

    Lee, Rigg. Worms—Love 'Em or Leave 'Em. New York: Pete Moss Publishers, 1982.

4. D. A. D'Longlegs interviewed by A. T. Leggs at 10 A.M. on October 26, 1999 in Marshy Bogg Swamp, Seattle, WA.

    D'Longlegs, D.A. Marshy Bogg Swamp, Seattle, WA, October 26, 1999.

5. Social Studies Teachers Can Win $5,000 Prize was an article found in the CD News-Bank, <u>The News & Observer</u> on September 27, 1996: B1. It was written by Thomas Jefferson Smith.

    Smith, Thomas Jefferson. "Social Studies Teachers Can Win $5,000 Prize." CD Newsbank. The News and Observer. Sept. 27, 1996.

6. The book, Living Without Electricity, was written by Steven Scott and Kenneth Pellman in 1990. It was published by Good Books in Pittsburgh.

    Scott, Steven and Kenneth Pellman. Living Without Electricity. Pittsburgh: Good Books, 1990.

7. Appearing in Vol. 22 of the Encyclopedia Britannica in the 1963 edition was an article on "Turkey," found on pages 193–205.

    "Turkey." Encyclopedia Britannica. Vol. 22, 1963: pp. 193–205.

8. I received an e-mail through Usenet entitled The Technical German on September 7, 1994. Thomas Michael Shaumann wrote it on August 5, 1994. It was received from Newsgroup comp.educ.languages.natural.

    Shaumann, Thomas Michael. "The Technical German." [Online] Available e-mail: Newsgroup comp.educ.languages.natural. Aug. 5, 1994.

9. Censorship, a book with David L. Bender as the editor, was written in 1985 in St. Paul and published by Greenhaven Press.

    Bender, David L., ed. Censorship. St. Paul: Greenhaven Press, 1985.

Bibliography Practice

Jennifer needs help writing a bibliographic list. She used the sources listed in the paragraph below while writing her research report: Does Birth Order Determine Personality?

In the book Family Constellation written by Walter Toman, Jennifer found information. The book was published in New York by Springer Publishing Company, Inc. in 1976. In The Birth Order Book published by Dell Publishing Company, Inc., in New York, she found information on pages 14–152. This book was written by Kevin Leman and published in 1985. Jennifer also read Sky Magazine in September 1985 where she found an article on pages 145–148 entitled "Personality by Position." In 1983, Cecile Ernst and Jules Angst wrote the book Birth Order which was published by Springer-Verlag in Berlin. Finally, Jennifer found an article in <u>Encyclopedia Americana</u> entitled "Birth Order," which appeared in 1987 in the B Volume on pages 77–79.

Bibliography

"Birth Order." Encyclopedia Americana. Vol. B, 1987: pp. 77–79.

Ernst, Cecile and Jules Angst. Birth Order. Berlin: Springer-Verlag, 1983.

Leman, Kevin. The Birth Order Book. New York: Dell Publishing Company, Inc., 1985.

"Personality by Position." Sky Magazine. September, 1985: pp. 145–148.

Toman, Walter. Family Constellation. New York: Springer Publishing Company, Inc., 1976.

Writing the Final Bibliography

It is now your turn to write a bibliography for your paper. Use the space provided below. Remember: When making the bibliography list: 1) put the list in alphabetical order according to the author's last name (if the author is not given, alphabetize by the first word in the title); 2) underline the title of books, encyclopedias, newspapers, and magazines; and 3) record the city, publishing company, and date of publication. Use pp. 50–51 for reference.

Bibliography

Answers will vary.

Note to the Teacher: Reproduce these title cards on card stock and give to each student who is doing a social studies project.

Social Studies Project Title Cards

PURPOSE

METHODOLOGY

CONCLUSION

GRAPH

CHART

DATA

SURVEY

111

Notes

_____

_____

_____

_____

_____

_____

_____

_____

_____

_____

_____

_____

_____

_____

_____

_____

_____

_____

_____

_____

_____